The Taciturn Man
and other Tales of Australia

Geoffrey Gibson

Foreword by Susan Violante

From the World Voices Series

Modern History Press

From the World Voices Series

Library of Congress Cataloging-in-Publication Data

Gibson, Geoffrey (Geoffrey Hope), 1937-
  The taciturn man : and other tales of Australia / Geoffrey Gibson.
    p. cm. -- (Modern voices series)
  ISBN 978-1-61599-120-4 (pbk. : alk. paper) -- ISBN 978-1-61599-121-1 (hardcover : alk. paper)
  1. Gibson, Geoffrey (Geoffrey Hope), 1937- 2. Gibson, Geoffrey (Geoffrey Hope), 1937---Childhood and youth. 3. Gibson, Geoffrey (Geoffrey Hope), 1937---Family. 4. Sydney (N.S.W.)--Biography. 5. Sydney (N.S.W.)--Social life and customs. 6. Double Bay (Sydney, N.S.W.)--Biography. 7. Double Bay (Sydney, N.S.W.)--Social life and customs. 8. Fathers and sons--Australia--Sydney (N.S.W.) 9. World War, 1939-1945--Australia--Sydney (N.S.W.) 10. Farm life--Australia--History--20th century. I. Title.
  DU178.G52 2011
  994.4'106092--dc23
  [B]
                                        2011035683

Modern History Press, an imprint of
Loving Healing Press
5145 Pontiac Trail
Ann Arbor, MI 48105

Tollfree USA/CAN 888-761-6268
London, UK

Distributed by Ingram Book Group (USA/CAN), Bertram's Books (UK),

Contents

Dedication

I wish to thank my dear friend Elizabeth Clarke who solves everyone's problems, and takes me surfing and is kind enough to say that I keep the sharks away.

Foreword

As the daughter of Italian Immigrants in Venezuela, I grew up exposed to immigrants' stories from relatives, friends, and even teachers. I loved listening to their stories as I grew up because they showed life at faraway places, during long passed eras, lived by previous generations. I would sit quietly imagining these grownups as young people going through so many things I would never live as they narrated out loud their anecdotes. I became curious about my own family stories as I began learning from how others experienced life. That is how my own book *Innocent War: Behind an Immigrant's Past Book 1* and the upcoming books of its series came to be.

After a lifetime of collecting life adventures from Immigrants in a narrative form, I found while writing *Innocent War* that there is something special about a life story when we listen to it as it is voiced out from its source. That is the part that I enjoyed as a child, that is the part that I love when I listen to my father's tapes or I interview him as I write my *Nino* series; that is the part that I loved the most of *The Taciturn Man and other Tales of Australia by Geoffrey Gibson.*

The Taciturn Man and other Tales of Australia is a collection of anecdotes in which Gibson shares his life through his humoristic and unique point of view. His words speak of times of struggle and times of ease as he recounts the different stages of his life through Australia's landscape and history. I loved meeting picturesque characters that left an imprint through Gibson's eyes. I enjoyed Gibson's ability to make me laugh through sad situations and how he warms my heart through the awkward ones.

Although I was impressed by Gibson's mastery of the written word, it is his candid and simple writing style that captivated me. *The Taciturn Man and other Tales of Australia* is not only a narrative of life in faraway places, and past eras. It does not only present a collection of life lessons through entertaining anecdotes. I found it to be much more than that as it not only shows us life, but also how this life was taken in by the author. Gibson delivers his point of view to the reader through the color of his words:

"In the bush, an Australian drought is an awesome thing; I have seen three. They arrived with great stealth, until, after several days of clear blue skies, we realized, always too late, that a drought has us in its grip. Everything seemed to happen in slow motion; the land changed from its verdant soft green hues to those of a harsh brown and yellow. The level in the dams sunk, as it did in the creeks, soaks, and water holes. Day by day, the cattle and sheep became thin and listless, as they scavenged, and slowly their feed disappeared. The sheep ran in search of dry clover seed to lick up, and the cattle foraged where they normally never would, and reached up to chew branches from edible trees."

His genuine candidness through his humor:

"...The other thing, before we get too deeply into the subject, I confess to having a liking for females in uniform. Don't ask me where that stems from, but nonetheless, it is there. You understand, therefore, that for me, a nicely proportioned lady, striding confidently forward, attired in what is now universally known as a 'power suit', has the completely opposite effect than what its wearer may have intended. Intimidated or impressed I am not; invariably attracted I am."

Geoffrey Gibson took me back to my parents' dinner table where we would listen to relatives and friends as their colorful voices delivered their life anecdotes through their personality, humor and picturesque story telling. And so I invite everyone to listen to this story teller as his colorful words come alive in *The Taciturn Man and other Tales of Australia*.

Susan Violante, September 2011

~~~

Susan Violante, is the author of *Innocent War: Behind and Immigrants Past Book 1*, a blogger, radio host of "I Have Something to Say Live", and editorial assistant for Reader Views and First Chapter Plus.

Part I -
Growing Up in Rural Australia

The Taciturn Man

In the bush, an Australian drought is an awesome thing; I have seen three. They arrived with great stealth, until, after several days of clear blue skies, we realized, always too late, that a drought has us in its grip. Everything seemed to happen in slow motion; the land changed from its verdant soft green hues to those of a harsh brown and yellow. The level in the dams sunk, as it did in the creeks, soaks, and water holes. Day by day, the cattle and sheep became thin and listless, as they scavenged, and slowly their feed disappeared. The sheep ran in search of dry clover seed to lick up, and the cattle foraged where they normally never would, and reached up to chew branches from edible trees.

The drought of this story happened in Australia, on a run-down bush block in the Uargon Valley. This was in the foothills of an ancient volcanic range known as "The Warrumbungles", which is in the State of New South Wales. This is midway between the towns of Gilgandra and Coonabarrabran and where that soft volcanic country rises from the surrounding plain.

The old timber and iron roofed homestead had two sources of water. When it rained, the roof collected our drinking water in two great tanks mounted on timber decks in the garden, which were just high enough so it naturally flowed through the house taps. The water for the garden, the laundry and bathing, and for the stock in the adjoining house paddock, came from a high overhead tank, which was filled from a windmill mounted over a bore. Day after relentless day, there were no clouds, and no rain, and increasingly more seriously, no wind; which meant no water was being pumped up the bore. The garden died, and disregarding the water desperately needed for the stock, we had to ration our own use of this precious resource.

The grass cover had all but disappeared; the dry stems broke and lay scattered in the dust; and the hardiest grasses were those varieties the stock would not touch. The clumps of red grass, tussock, and spear grass turned yellow, and they and the grey coarse saffron and scotch thistle survived, but apart from them, the land seemed dead. In the morning and at night, we listened to news on the radio, particularly for the weather forecast, and searched the sky for any sign of a change.

City people are often amused by the country person's preoccupation with the weather, for they would not have seen when great clouds of red dust billowed in from the west and laid a fine layer over everything, nor would they know of a water shortage or have listened to an iron-roof creak and groan in the stifling heat.

'G'day Bert, how are you going? Dry over our way,' the locals might say in their slow and deliberate country way.

'Yeah Charlie, and I reckon it is over where we are. No sign of rain; we haven't had a drop for months and our land is just blowing away.'

'Go on Bert. I sold a mob of cows the other day. I couldn't afford to keep them. I took twenty-five quid a head from a bloke who had feed over on the coast, and the stock agent reckoned I was lucky.'

Each day began with the sun rising in a red blaze over the hills as it came blasting through my open bedroom door in what may have been a personal wake-up call. Outside, the earth was still, bare, brown, and dead; it still retained the warmth from the day before. In a nearby paddock, sheep bleated and milled around in their hunger; and above my head, the corrugated iron roof expanded with a harsh cracking and tearing. The sun, heat, and the wind may work together, but there is another dimension to a drought that I recall, which began in a violent, dry, electrical storm that sent lightning flashes and wind-driven fire leaping across the land.

As the drought worsened, the old sheep and cows died first; they simply sat down where they were and never got up. The newborn lambs might stand up but they never sucked, while over the fence, the ploughed clods turned to dust. The farmers joked and yarned together in a stoic attempt to disguise their worry. They purchased expensive feed for their starving stock, and they had to ask themselves *when do you begin* and *when do you stop*, or *should I begin at all?* But of course they cared; and of course they paid for feed, and, in despair, watched their mounting debt to the bank grow.

Not quite panic stations, but all luxuries, holidays, even the occasional trips to town were cancelled, and each day became a battle. Selling all the stock was not an option. Who in a drought, when it was as severe and as widespread as this one, could possibly want to run a herd of aged bone-thin cows or a mob of starving ewes?

A drought is like a never-ending story in which the hurdles put in the way of the principal character are never actually overcome, not before they are replaced by new ones. Australian artists have captured the faces of country women; they have that lost, drained-of-expression look, which has their private struggle etched upon them. It is a peculiarly Australian look, where the eyes stare into the distance, there is never a hint of a smile, and one wonders if it signifies a begrudging acceptance.

Our routine was to cut the edible Kurrajong brush from morning till night to feed the stock, while all the time the starved animals milled around the valley below. We cleaned out the springs and soaks, and dug in among the rocks and sand to make small water holes where the stock might drink. In the meantime, the precious household drinking water sank lower and lower, as did the water from the bore during the spells of windless days. At night, we listened to music and read, and talked about what we would do when it rained. There were certainly, for me, intensely private moments, when I wondered will it ever rain; or could this be the final reckoning; or have I... have we sinned, and incurred the great creator's wrath; and what if it never does rain? And that was only my second drought.

People write of a soldier's courage, of endurance against the greatest odds, of men and women who could have been expected to succumb, but never did. I have never seen or want to see a war, and yet I have seen a long fought battle. I have certainly seen the courage and endurance of our country people.

But as the people in and around that valley would recall, on Christmas day, a searing bushfire broke out in a paddock not that far. There were extraordinary scenes, and not many meters away, a wiry man, on whose farm we had come to establish a front, was engaged in his own private battle against wind and fire. At the very best, all we could hope to do was to try and contain it, which, in the end, although we kept at it, we were only moderately successful in doing. Here and there, it raced away out into the open country; it was incredible that it could, as there was little but the bare earth left to burn.

The stoic and lone, battling farmer is not a myth, and I can still see that wiry farmer with his head of thick curly grey hair, grey trousers, long-sleeved Bushman shirt, braces, and a thick belt. For this man was suddenly gripped by an unstoppable need to do something, anything. Hot wind blew in howling gusts and burning dung raced across the earth, setting fire to anything it touched, until the very ground seemed to be burning. Nearby, the hollow grey trunk and branches of an old dead gum tree were burning fiercely and spewing red hot ashes high into the air, as if escaping a chimney, and it was obvious that when it finally fell, it would fall across a netting fence.

I was standing by, so that, as the embers fell on the fence line, it was my job to put out any burning fence post with a knapsack spray. When, with the look of someone at their wit's end, the wiry farmer slammed the back of his axe into that burning trunk, we watched mesmerized by the crazed futility of it; and he did it again, and was once more covered in a cascade of burning ash. He was pulled away, rolled on the ground, and his burning hair and clothing smothered.

But how I ended up fire fighting in that valley is part the story of my coming to manhood, and getting to know my father. Alexander was born in 1905 and died in 1965 and his army enlistment papers of 1940 describe him as a thirty-five-year-old grocer. There were similar circumstances to those of that writer. I was three when Alexander went to war, and an eight-year-old boy when he came home.

To call him a reserved and taciturn Englishman does not go nearly far enough to reveal the father I discovered. Not quite eccentric, but certainly he was different. He was educated at Queens College in Taunton, Somerset, and as a young man, my father and his brother came to Australia. I later found out that their mother (Jenny Gibson) had divorced and remarried, and also that her sons had left England largely because of that; I imagine they arrived here with a sense of adventure.

I am also not sure which came first, the marriage of Alec and his brother Arthur to two sisters, who were Jane and Alma Solomon, or their purchase of two sheep grazing blocks. I know Jane and Alec married on December 24th, 1929 and despite a search, I was never able to find their block, which was known as "Cressbrook". Suffice to say that it nestled in the then untamed hills of New England, somewhere out from the city of Inverell. I believe that my uncle Arthur and Alma lived about thirty or so miles away near the village of Nullamana.

Years ago, and long after he and my mother had lived their lives, and in a nostalgic whim to revisit the past, I had set out on a private pilgrimage to find where they had lived. I had heard the vague family stories; I knew it was known as "Cressbrook", but that was about all. I never did find it, although I drove up an endless dirt track which carved into the side of steep hills. I asked at isolated farms and a village post office, where I met an old man who reckoned he remembered them.

The country and the track were so rough, I wondered how they ever drove in and out; yet they must have; their three children were definitely conceived and born while they were there. That would have been in the early and mid-nineteen thirties, before the days of modern road graders, and in a Model "T" Ford, a car he nostalgically talked about. Nearly forty years later, and in my modern car, I eventually gave up and turned back. After an endless and bewildering succession of gates, and difficult to follow directions, I had only arrived at a dead-end paddock. Finding where they had lived obviously needed more research, and was a project for another day.

I have my recollections of his mother, a thin, very English and tweedy sort of woman. My father did say he had sold toilet paper in Farmers, a snooty Sydney department store where he had to wear a stiff collar and a suit. Presumably, he sold my mother a roll or two, which must have pleased her, and may have eventually led to the joining of the two families.

When the Second World War ended, the flying boat service to England was resumed, and his mother used to fly out in a great lumbering machine that landed, like a fat pelican, in the middle of Sydney Harbor. On one memorable visit, she arrived in the middle of a scorching Sydney summer, dressed presumably just as she had boarded, which would have been in the middle of England's winter. Anyway, the poor lady was wearing a heavy brown Harris Tweed suit with a fox stole around her neck, and matching felt hat pinned to her hair. In my eyes, she was very grand; her hair, when it was uncovered, was swept up and held in place by a brown tortoise-shell comb pinned at the back. Children are perceptive; I may have been nine or ten at the time, but my brother, sister, and I immediately picked up the vibes; we sensed that for some unknown reason, our parents were intimidated by her presence.

After the two brothers married the sisters, they ended up living in the hills around Inverell. But I had often wondered how they ended up on those isolated grazing blocks, and the very strangeness of it. I came up with a simple explanation, which is this: there had been a catastrophic worldwide economic depression in 1929, and the brothers would have probably been retrenched, along with everyone else, from selling toilet paper, or whatever they were doing at the time.

I surmised that to solve the problem of making her sons successful breadwinners, their mother had stepped in to fill the gaps. That theory fits, even though, to my knowledge, neither she nor her boys had any experience with rural life in Australia. It could have happened through the London head office of one of the great pastoral houses, which were very prominent financial institutions in Australia in those days. She would have simply ordered two small grange blocks suitable for raising sheep and cattle, one for each son, and did so from halfway around the world, completely, as they say in the business, "sight unseen".

Having been in the property field myself, I could imagine the salesmen of the Sydney office combing through their books for two of the roughest places which they had not been able to give away, let alone sell. To them, it would have seemed like the Gods of the property world had suddenly smiled down upon them, and a miracle had occurred. Hence the trouble in finding where my mother and father, hopefully in a moment of pleasure, was good enough to conceive me. It all seemed to make sense, and to be as likely a theory as any other.

But that Great Depression lingered and had certainly humbled Australia. Then a terrible family tragedy happened; a crippling disease struck my father's brother, whom I was to come to know as my uncle Arthur. So by 1940, both properties had been sold, I would think for very little, and the sisters (my mum and my aunt Alma) were running corner grocery stores in Sydney, and Alexander had joined the army.

To take a distant, if cynical, view of it, I think the Second World War may have in some way rescued my father. He had left our mother to fend for herself and their three children, which sounds very melodramatic now, but in those days was what happened to the wives of men who joined up. However, she was a woman ahead of her time, and she successfully ran her corner store in Double Bay. It was a thriving business when her husband returned.

In a way, my generation got a second-hand view of the Great Depression, and of World War II. The first made our parents very cautious, particularly of any expense; its effects could always be seen in their lives. There were random snippets of it; how their wool was not worth two pence, and how they used it to fill the potholes in their access road. They became frugal in everything; you could see it in the way they talked to others who had been through it; who were exactly the same, worn down and chastened by it.

Typical of his generation, my father rarely spoke about the war. When a journalist friend of his, who was in the same unit, wrote a book about their wartime experiences, he described my father as being a man of few words. When he returned from the army, I came to know a distant, wiry man, who was very proud of Winston Churchill. For Alexander could perform his better-known speeches, not quite capturing the voice, but rekindling the same rousing and stentorian tone.

But alas, there he was—returned from the war and stuck in a corner shop, serving up three pennies worth of pork fritz, together with their carefully measured ration of butter, jam, bacon, tea, and sugar to over-picky, suburban housewives. Most things were rationed; if not, they were in short supply, which certainly applied to cigarettes, which were sold with much favoritism and secrecy, from under the counter.

Alexander found himself enclosed by the piddling world of grocery transactions and delivering car loads of their phone orders, to the posh households of Double Bay, Darling Point, and Bellevue Hill, where, perhaps the husband had made his fortune, while my father and Winston Churchill had been fighting the Hun and the "Nips", as the Japanese were called in wartime disparagement.

Then in another mystery, almost as completely incomprehensible as how they had ended up living in the wilds of those barren hills before the war, my father disappeared briefly. He quietly and shyly slipped away and later announced upon his return, that he had purchased a bush block where he proposed to live. With a flair for the dramatic, he never said how heavily timbered it was, or that it was not far removed from those very same barren hills of New England, as we were to discover later.

But prior to this, his wife's brother, who had been captured by the Japanese, had come back from the war as thin as a blade of grass, and very damaged. He was my uncle Rick, who was then recovering and while he did, he spent his days helping in the shop. Well, let us say, he and my father spent most of their time helping my mother in the shop, in between ducking up to the nearby pub during the day for an ale or two. They would have escaped the demands of returned life, and to be out of reach of those demanding housewives.

If you can imagine a time when there were no supermarkets, such suburban corner shops, or "emporiums", as he grandly called theirs, did very well. My father had acquired a dark-green 1928 Chrysler motorcar with a high square cabin, leather bench seats, timber spoked wheels and a spare wheel mounted on the rear. There were no new cars in those years, and this one had been kept up on bricks in the elderly owner's garage for the duration of the war, when there had been no petrol for private use anyway. So it happened one day that my father and the 1928 Chrysler disappeared. Not much was said; we went to school; and our mother continued to run the shop.

I next caught up with my father very late on a freezing night on Walcha Road railway platform. I would be unsure if he and the 1928 Chrysler were going to make it out of his bush block, hidden somewhere in the cold hills of New England. Sometimes they did not, and the stationmaster, used to this sort of thing, would turn up with a mug of tea and stoke up the waiting room fire. He would have received a phone call from my father that he was delayed, and would then organize yet another misplaced schoolboy onto the bus heading for the town of Walcha, where, if it was not too late and the Greek café was open, I could have a plate of ham and eggs with tea, until he turned up.

Alexander would have been bogged, had a puncture, or the car had overheated and refused to go, any one of a dozen problems you could have with rough, unmade roads, and a very old car. His country idyll was different; at places, the trees were so close that, looking up, it was difficult to see the sky, and their trunks were so thick that it would have taken a dozen schoolboys to stretch around them. A stream, with banks of tangled blackberries, and trout and platypuses living in it, ran just below the house and joined the MacDonald River downstream.

The previous owner, who also must have been at least mildly eccentric, had lived pretty rough, but not so rough as to stop him from carving out three passable golf holes, each with their own short fairways and greens, out of this wilderness. There was an outside toilet, which was only a flat timber seat suspended above a deep hole. This had a faded red faded-red timber outhouse built over it, the whole thing being sited well away from the house and beyond the garden fence. He used to boast that his outhouse faced east and caught the morning sun. There was no plumbing, and water from the kitchen sink drained straight into a bucket.

The rolling hills had old gold mine workings and were covered in bracken and extensive rabbit warrens. Foxes trailed their tails behind as they scampered over logs, and peered dimly at intruders. On an adjoining block among the trees lived a retired Indian tea planter and his wife, with whom Alexander had struck up a friendship. The men would sit on the veranda, sip scotch and water, and talk. My father would tell of grand schemes, such as clearing a paddock and planting it with potatoes.

None of this was lost on an impressionable boy, but stored away to be vividly recalled during Greenwood's English, or a testy Mr. Porter's Latin declensions, during which might come pleasant recollections of three white horses, roped one behind the other, the leading one being ridden by an old man named Percy Clair, who had a spectacular handlebar moustache. When he was there, Percy lived in a rough hut and ate nothing but tins of herrings in tomato sauce. He and his fat white horses would appear like an apparition, winding through the trees. There were also memories of ducks swimming in the river, or the thumps and delight of wallabies and kangaroos bounding through the timber.

Over several valleys and hills away, the tea planter had a brother, a retired surgeon, who lived with his wife and made wonderful trout flies. He and his brother, fished the rivers and streams for miles around, and kept sheep that wandered unhurriedly about, and red and white cattle, that looked very cold in winter. Alexander also kept sheep and some cattle, some of which strayed, a state of affairs about which he seemed unconcerned.

He would set off on an old horse and with a black and white border collie named "Smoky" trailing behind, which, for some unknown reason, he would swear dreadfully at. They would go off into the trees, looking for his lost stock, and on his return, he would accept that some may have wandered off through a broken fence, died of worms or liver fluke, fallen down a mine shaft, or simply succumbed to the harsh conditions or old age.

He kept hens, milked a cow, killed a fowl every now and then, which, roasted or stewed, were tougher than old boots, perhaps because he was working his way through the older ones first. Upon reflection, I think he liked living alone. He would butcher a sheep, give the offal to his dogs, and hang the carcass overnight under a tree, and in the morning, cut up the meat and store it in the kerosene refrigerator. The lamb was delicious. I don't think we children ever thought of our holidays with him as living rough. In my mind, those times are stored away as a boy's adventure.

II

Disregarding my fond remembrances, and despite the severe downsides of my father's life, and there had been a few, luck finally sort him out. Quite suddenly, and through absolutely nothing to do with anything he had done, his plot of land—his personal retreat from selling groceries to the fussy ladies of Double Bay, his strange and hidden block in the timbered hills of New England—became worth a fortune. Perhaps it was his guardian angel making up for his previous experiences among sparser cold hills. Truly a fortune, with or without its rabbit warrens, his straggled woolly sheep, and lonely cattle, lost or found, they and his faded red outhouse, slop bucket, two old horses and one much-sworn-at Border Collie, had suddenly become a fabled lode of gold.

The fierce Korean War of 1949, fought in the freezing snow in that difficult country, had caused a tremendous wool boom. There was a mad scramble for land where fine wool sheep could graze, and his country was the most sought-after land of all. This was cold, high country, where the sheep grew a fine, clean wool, of the type much favored for making warm clothing.

All this sudden wealth had some unforeseen results; my mother suddenly sold their emporium, and would take us for a family holiday to stay with him during the longer school breaks. The 1928 green, square Chrysler had disappeared, and a brand new British-made Vanguard utility truck met us at the station. The slop bucket had gone, and on winter mornings, there was hot water on tap. There were new clothes for everyone, and a grey Ferguson tractor with a three-point linkage and a moldboard plough stood under the trees, ready for planting potatoes, should he wish or ever get around to, which he never did.

The tea famer's wife held nice parties, as did the surgeon's, for which I was scrubbed, neatly pressed and severely lectured on how to behave. My elder sister was matched with a ruddy cheeked farmer's son, who got up at five on frosty mornings and could drive a truck, castrate a calf, and who each day milked four cows before breakfast.

But of my father, despite all his sudden affluence, in the back of his mind, there was the vivid memory of The Great Depression, of being dirt-poor, and using wool to fill the pot holes. Then, in a move that was a worthy imitation of one of Churchill's great wartime conferences, he acted. One evening, and this is exactly as I recall it, he and the prospective buyers were seated on cane chairs around a matching glass-topped table with a jug of iced water and a bottle of scotch in the middle.

During this negotiation, which took place in the enclosed front sunroom, he sold out to some very eager neighbors. They were men with hearty laughs and booming country voices, who had suddenly appeared with a large new truck, which was equal in length to the width of the whole front garden. They had driven in from their block further down the track, from somewhere out among the trees. The result of this Churchillian negotiation will lead us elsewhere.

III

As I was to discover, he had an affinity with steep hills and, years later as a result of that earlier sale, he purchased another block. This parcel was very rundown and had perpendicular hills, the more level parts of which were covered with saffron and scotch thistle, and every other noxious weed known to mankind. This new tumbledown block had, in his eyes, a major fault: the outside toilet faced due west. But in all other respects, it was a repeat of the last privy, except that the walls were of painted-green, corrugated iron. But in no way was that the only fault; and it seems I may have unwittingly had a hand in all of this. Some of his strange ways must have been inherited, or perhaps had just scraped off on me.

I should explain that I had long left home and that, when last seen, my parents had returned from a long sea voyage to Europe. My father had settled into a job selling spare parts in a section of a car dealership in Rushcutters Bay, and in all respects, he seemed to have settled into suburban life.

By then I was a young man of around nineteen or twenty. I had completed my compulsory military training and had gone out into the sheep country of Central Queensland. There, in some distant and nostalgic reaction to that late forties' wool boom, I was working with a sheep shearing contractor. At the time, in my eyes anyway, I was getting valuable experience, and I had recently completed a course in sheep husbandry and wool classing, which I now worked at as I travelled around the shearing sheds.

Then tiring of going from shed to shed and living rough like a gypsy, I got a job on a large and very well-run rural property. This was to do all the jobs any ordinary person was too sensible to do. This work was known as "jackerooing", but was really a euphemism for doing cheap labor in return for living with the owner's family, and hopefully being trained in the rural life. This was far away from those cold, remote hills of my father's former haunts; this was warm country, about farming broad acres of wheat, lucerne, maize, barley and oats. It was all about well-laid-out and watered paddocks, perfectly maintained fences, weed control, animal husbandry, and knowing where all the sheep and cattle were most of the time.

Whenever I was home in Sydney, our father was always affable and took my brother and me out for a beer, to the cricket, the football, or, on Sunday mornings, to Bondi Beach for a surf. My sister had married and my brother was beavering away with his girlfriend and attending law school. I had talked glowingly to the family of my life, and written them long, winded letters about how rich the western country was. Full of how big the sheep grew, how much wool they produced, and how much better they thrived in the hotter country out on the western plains.

I had, in fact, been referring to the great rolling western plain that stretches in all directions, toward a spur of his former range of hills in the east, and to the vague rest of Australia somewhere in the west. But even out there, in all its vastness, and in something to be admired, and unknown to me, he had managed to find and buy some impressive untamed hills. This new idyll, his new rundown block with perpendicular hills and acres of useless grey, dry thistle, deep-eroded gullies, and countless rabbits, had a few other surprises too.

But there is something mystical, idealistic, and adventurous, and I think even pure, about the eagerness of young men to go where they have not been and to do things they have not yet done. There was something irresistible about the thought of joining my father for his new adventure. Perhaps it was because he was not around when I was a boy. So I wrote to ask if I could; my letter would have said I had learned a great deal, and that I thought I would be able to help.

And certainly there are times in everyone's life when you move on to the next challenge. Much to my delight, he agreed, which is how I came to be fighting a bush fire on that Christmas day, and had watched that wretched neighbor accidentally set himself on fire in his despair. For the rest of that summer, we waited for the call to fight a fire, but it was the hot westerly wind we feared, which burnt everything before it, as if the land had just exploded.

That Christmas day had been a traditional family gathering. He had made a ceremony, serving sliced ham with mustard and beer first thing in the morning with his sons, one of the charming little idiosyncrasies he had invented. Then an hour or two before lunch, more beer was served, and there was a rousing Churchillian speech delivered from the rear veranda. It was so hot during lunch that we cooled down several times under the garden hose, and as the main course was drawing to a close, we were called out to fight a fire.

When we arrived, two houses in the nearby village of Tooraweenah, which, in the native tongue, ominously means "a place of many brown snakes", were well alight. You could say one had already gone, and there was considerable upset and confusion. We had removed everything we could out of the surviving house, until some fool opened the rear door, and with the wind ripping in behind it and, with a fierce whoosh, the fire roared right through and out the front door. Meanwhile, either in panic or it may have even been the same person, but stupidly, shots were fired into an overhead water tank standing in the rear garden, but to no avail, as only a few pathetic driblets of water fell from it.

When the burned-out families had been resettled with their neighbors—and there was nothing more to be done—with red eyes, and very dry and hot, we adjourned to the "Mountain View", the village pub, to continue the festivities. No sooner was the first beer in our hands, than we were called out again. This time a bush fire was moving on a wide front from west to east, and rolling across the bare paddocks a few miles down the valley from the scene of our lunch. When we arrived, the remaining old grass as well as the dry pellets of sheep and rabbit dung were well alit and being blown along the bare ground by a hot westerly; so they set fire to virtually anything they touched.

In the back of our minds, certainly in mine, was the fear that apart from a corrugated iron roof, our home was built of the local, highly flammable cypress pine, and that if it caught fire, it would explode. The summer of that year left me with memories of fires, hot west winds and huge dust storms, dead or dying stock, the loss of a garden, and the countryside turning to dust.

When I joined him, my father was living much like a recluse, and had a few personal things in what was eventually to be a living room in the middle of the house. All the rooms were just bare boards with rough timber-lined ceilings and walls, and he had reduced his life to the basic essentials. I camped in a small room on the eastern side which caught the morning sun. All up, we had a couple of beds, a kitchen table, two or three chairs, a few wooden boxes, an old green metal meat safe, kerosene lamps, and not much else.

The kitchen had a fuel stove with green enameled doors; wood for it was no trouble, as there was plenty of that lying about in the house paddock. On winter evenings, we would set an open fire in the living room. He was an interesting and amusing man to live with, and there were shades of his former army life. 'Reveille,' he would say, using the military terminology, 'will be at 0600 hours, when troops will move out with water bags, axes, pliers, wire strainers, shovels, crowbars, and fencing wire, as issued, "troops for the use of". Then they will march out in column of route to go fencing.' But in the morning, there would be leisurely and copious cups of tea, and his angle on the world, given while listening to the radio news, and having lamb chops, toast and fried eggs for breakfast.

My father could be a wonderful conversationalist, and he had a view on most things. Although, if he chose, he could be aloof, and difficult to get to know, in that very reserved English way. He was a man with a singular nature, who kept a stiff upper lip in any private anguish, nor was he given to praise, although there were times when he let it known that he was not displeased with whatever it was I had done. Generally, I felt he was happy that I was there, although it would have been nice if he had expressed it. But he was my father, was good company, and in my eyes could do little wrong.

My mother, who had stayed in Sydney, was a compulsive letter writer, although she never said anything of any great moment; yet her letters arrived in a steady stream and were full of motherly advice. He rarely wrote to his children, perhaps a short reply, and, as we were taught, using the phone was an extravagance, so that if you were not there on the spot, you never saw or heard from him.

The Great Depression was the great influence on his life, his memory of it never far away, so the meager equipment, the tools, with which he proposed to run his sheep and cattle venture on that steep and strange-shaped block of land, were almost nonexistent. There were those I have mentioned, which anyone with a suburban garden might own, add to them one duck-egg-blue Holden car, one of the first models built by General Motors in Australia after the war, and there was nothing more.

Straight up those vertical hills we marched; there were so many deep-eroded gullies, so much thick saffron thistle, and the country so steep, that in the early days, the car was of very little use. We discovered that at places, roughly every hundred meters, the boundary fence, which may have been the original, had a tree lying across it, or had been flattened by the kangaroos, which, up until then, had had the place to themselves. Our routine was one of tramping out and fence repair, and to me, each day was one of discovery. I think that in the early days, although he never said so, he may have been a bit overawed, as I certainly was, at what he had taken on.

That boundary fence line was discussed in detail, sometimes with much amusement, and other times, with a curse. We reckoned it must have been determined years ago, by an underpaid government clerk, whom we pictured sitting in his city office, perhaps an earnest fellow, who would have had no idea of the havoc he was wreaking as he drew those boundary lines. They went straight up and down hills, over deep valleys and cliffs, without any concession to geography, nature, man, or beast.

While we were fence mending, I saw a side of my father I had no idea existed. We patched, propped up, and much to my surprise, I found he had the bushman's unique capacity to improvise, by making do with what was on hand, and was more energetic and determined than I had expected. All the time I was there, and although we made huge improvements, that boundary fence needed continuous checking and work to keep it stock-proof. There were few internal fences, and fortunately the most serviceable one, which ran roughly across the contour of the foothills, separated the slopes from the hills, and was in a reasonable order.

During our fencing, and to vary each day's work, we began a feat of ingenuity I still marvel at. We made tracks for the car through the bush, and got it in and out of impossible places, and in later years, those tracks proved very useful. And where we could not cross an eroded water course, we made detours around the head of gullies. But there was one deeply eroded chasm which literally cut the place in two. There was no way around its head. So during the cool of the day, we began to build a bridge over it. We used pine logs felled from a nearby stand of trees, and which we fastened together with plenty of 8 gauge wire.

After much toil, this bridge was finished, and, very gingerly and with him proudly standing by, I drove the car across. That was quite an occasion, and after a brief Churchillian speech, he declared the bridge open; and that night, we celebrated with a few beers. It really was a big deal; we could drive stock across it and it saved a major detour. However, during a heavy summer storm a few years later, it was washed away into the gully, where it still did valuable service by halting the erosion. We continued making tracks, including one memorable one cut around the head of a previously impassable gully. Years later, thinking of that experience reminded me of his stories of how he got his Model T Ford in and out of those steep cold hills of New England. It was then that I realized it was no wonder that I had not been able to find his first block where his children had been conceived.

Around that time, it had been very dry further out west around Nyngan. For having made the place reasonably stock proof, we went out to buy our first mob of sheep, and I have to say that they and their owner looked decidedly worn-out to me. But that great economic recession of before the war would not let go 'if we can get a couple of lambs out of these,' Alexander said, 'they will not owe us a thing,' and apart from dropping dead from the ordeal, they never did.

Acquiring that mob of elderly ewes was why I hastily set out to find a sheepdog. All such searches should be commenced in a pub, which was as far as I had to go. There in the bar of The Mountain View Hotel, in the nearby village of Tooraweenah, I was told that if I headed out along the dusty road to Coonamble, I would meet an old drover with a large mob of sheep, whom, I was assured, had a young dog for sale.

And so he did. The drover was an old Swede named Jorgensen and his puppy was a red and white crossbred kelpie, tethered on a line so it trotted along underneath the drover's surprisingly elaborate wagon. There were two horses, one in the shafts, the other tethered behind, and a great mob of woolly sheep stretched out along the stock route in front. Over a billy of tea, very little money and an interesting chat, including a few handy tips on dog training, and the assurance that the pup had the right instinct and would soon be ready to work, I acquired a wonderful dog I called "Danny". He was named that after a very good stock horse it had been my pleasure to ride as a jackaroo.

The Uargon Valley has a distinctive rock formation at its head, variously known as the "Spire" or the "Bread Knife" and when I saw its blue peak in the distance, I knew I was home. The locals said it was the core of an extinct volcano, one of many in the Warrumbungle Mountains which was eroded by the rains, had spread their soft volcanic black soil out on the plains below. The rich top soil was full of dormant seed, and when it rained, a covering of paddy melons, clover, grass, and wild flowers miraculously appeared almost overnight.

After the initial shock of seeing his idyll for the first time, I came to love the place. The slopes were covered in Stringy Bark, Apple Gum, and Box trees, whose tiny flowers the bee farmers followed with their with hives. This was country, where practically for nothing, other than somewhere to camp and a feed, the axe men of the depression years had ring barked practically every tree on those slopes, and moved on like a plague of marauding locusts.

They had left their mark, and the hollow trunks of once living trees were left standing stark and grey, as though they had been cast in steel, and the broken remains of branches lay just where they had fallen. This was still a place where Western Red Kangaroos appeared timidly in the patches of remaining timber, and grey wallabies scrambled about among the rocky hills. Stands of Cypress pine stood upright on the slopes in their own patches of sandy red soil. In the summer months, brown snakes basked and slid away to their hiding places under a log, or like a length of hose, would disappear down a rabbit hole. Over on the north western side of the range, where the soil was sandy yellow, there was a never-ending and monotonous forest of Cypress called the "Pilliga Scrub", which regularly exploded into fires, after summer lightening strikes.

I also came to know a soft valley tucked away in the fringes of the range. It has the lovely sounding Aboriginal name of "Goorianawa" and it is a hidden, tranquil, and fertile place where I hunted wild pigs, which burrowed beneath the fences, and made their muddy wallows.

A normal year brought an extraordinary array of sight and color. During the wheat harvest, pink and white cockatoos gathered and played where the seed fell, and ate till they could barely move. The less greedy birds and new arrivals, wheeled and screeched so that, from a distance, the trees appeared to be draped in pink and white crepe.

When the land was fallow, if it had been farmed too often, it made its own protest by sprouting a thick covering of prickly scotch and saffron thistles, as if to say, "enough is enough; let me rest." Park-like, and appearing strangely out-of-place, dark-leafed Kurrajong trees, whose foliage the sheep, cattle, kangaroos and rabbits ate, were the recognizable signs of fertile country.

Their numbers in those days were declining, the valuable trees being destroyed by over lopping for fodder, attacked by wood borers and other tree pests; then of course, since the arrival of the white man, by overgrazing, when the young trees could not survive the teeth of foraging animals. One day, when I was eating my lunch in the shade of a tree, a kookaburra, sitting above, dropped a small brown snake right beside me, and before the dazed snake or I could react, the bird had swooped down and taken it up again to finish its meal.

Everywhere, and from dawn till dusk, there came the mournful cry of crows, which perched on the grey limbs of dead trees, from where they watched everything below. Nature's wonderful scavengers, were always waiting for a weakened sheep. Sometimes, they even took the eyes before it was dead. After which their prey might be finished off by the wedge-tail eagles that rode high above. On the ground, teary-eyed anteaters slowly wobbled through the tussocks and curled themselves into balls at the slightest footfall;

their brown and white quills hid them in the grass and repelled any curious animal.

After the harvest, the dust of tractors hung in the air, and the light was so bright that its reflection from the yellow ground was dazzling. At noon, the iron roofs and drums groaned in the scorching heat, and nothing moved. At night, riding home from a back paddock, the moon and stars lit everything, every tree, every rock exposed, as if from a gently filtered overhead light. After dusk, this took away the colors of the day, and left soft shadowy images in a wondrous landscape.

This is so fragile a place where, until the coming of the white man, for many thousands of years, humans have barely left their mark. The passing of the original inhabitants in the soft valleys and slopes of this ancient mountain range has largely gone unrecorded. I think that perhaps that is the very best of epitaphs.

IV

Coming from a highly organized and well-equipped farming operation, I found my father's frugal ways an irritant. However, I threw myself into doing everything his way, and in doing so learnt how to do a lot with very little. But seasons came and went, the ewes had lambs, the cows had calves, and the sheep grew wool. The fences were repaired, but there were still rabbits everywhere, as well as acres and acres of the best land which, in some distant time, had been cultivated, and were then covered in an impenetrable waist-high cover of dry thistles, which, apart from making a paddock useless, gave the sheep the awful sores of "scabby mouth".

With Alexander's background, getting him to buy anything was like trying to get money from a bank manager who did not want your business in the first place. All my father could see was his money floating away, a bit like leaves down a flooded creek. I knew about farming and what had to be done, and I had talked to our neighbors, and, bit by bit, I wore him down. But it was hard going, at every opportunity I produced newspaper clippings of second-hand tractors and ploughs and kept hammering away.

The memory still makes me shake my head in wonder. The result of all my badgering was an early 1920's International Harvester kerosene tractor, and a six-disk plough, both of which would have been better in a museum. Acquiring these may sound like a major purchase, but seen in its best light, it can be best explained this way: purchasing those two ancient implements was as ridiculous as buying an old suburban manual lawnmower to cut all the grass in the garden city of Canberra.

Everyone to their own delights, but at the time, being young and eager, I was thrilled to have his agreement, and after much work on both, including the fitting of two new rear tractor tires, we were getting there. Those tires were so expensive they caused a major rift. But that was not all; there were pails of grease, drums of fuel and oil, the fitting of new disks to the plough, the manufacture by a blacksmith of a suitable hitch, and we were ready to go. Despite these disparaging comments, once it was moving, we kept that old tractor rolling night and day.

Country people are different, and we were blessed with the most wonderful and generous neighbors, who, seeing what was happening, kept a straight face and offered only friendly encouragement. One in particular, a very industrious wheat farmer called Bob, a natural bush mechanic, would hear when the old tractor had stopped and would come over to see what the trouble was. Inevitably, he would end up staying to work on it, often late into the night, which happened with embarrassing frequency.

Alexander, once, in a moment of deep emotional passion, had gone forward in front of a whole sports stadium full of people to give himself, if only temporarily, to Jesus Christ. This had been at one of those emotionally charged Billy Graham crusades which had been very popular at the time. Now let me say there is nothing like the look or smell of newly turned damp earth to turn a man's passion to farming. Stranger things have happened, and before I knew it, I had a convert. Over the years, patches of cultivation appeared like painted landscapes, in between the gullies, on the slopes, on the top of, and in between those vertical hills.

Car tracks sprang up leading to out-of-the-way places to make a new patch of cultivation. The equipment level had expanded, what with grease pumps, and other basic tools needed for tractor maintenance. By then we had three sheep dogs, but still only one pony. My father remained impressed, and I am pleased to remember, that in time the old tractor and plough rested in well-earned retirement, where they were last parked under a Kurrajong tree.

I had purchased a pony from a farmer thirty miles away, and in keeping with the family memory of The Great Depression, I rode it home. My previous boss had been a very horsey fellow and I had been given a champion cattle-drafting horse to ride. This meant the horse taught me how to work cattle, rather than the other way around. We had badly needed the pony, because, as well as snakes and thistles, his hilly idyll came with a poisonous native plant the effect of which on sheep or cattle was the animal equivalent of having smoked several joints of marihuana, while at the same time having drunk the best part of a bottle of whiskey.

This plant has the common name of "Darling Pea"; it contained a narcotic with a most distressing effect on addicted animals. A neighbor had the side of his horse gored when it was charged by a pea-intoxicated cow. It was no fun, and I sprayed patches of it with very toxic chemicals, which I am sure did more harm to me than it did to the pea. Ah, the value of wise neighbors, after consultation with those who knew, we devised a new and very cunning plan.

Instead of keeping the stock away from it, we mustered every animal we had, and shepherded them onto a patch so that as many as possible became addicted. After a time of eating like something possessed them, there was not a sign of it left. That simple discovery was a fantastic breakthrough.

Around that time, there had been a revolution in broad acre farming and we had realized things had to change. Still, hardly spending a cent, except for fertilizer and seed, we entered into an arrangement with a sharecropper who had the latest in farming plant. He could farm more in a day than I could, if I had kept going night and day for three weeks.

This overcame the problem of lacking any modern machinery; also, he provided the labor. Part of the deal was that in the third year, he was to undersow the wheat crop with lucerne. This happy arrangement eventually converted paddocks full of thistle to lush green lucerne, and enabled us to fatten lambs and cattle for market after bringing them in from the hills.

But each evening, the rabbits gambled, fornicated endlessly, and ate everything in sight. I no longer had to drive our ancient tractor around in never-ending circles. And I had been saved from the ear-splitting din of four enormous cylinders banging away three feet from my ears, and an exhaust belching black kerosene smoke directly into my face. This release enabled us to declare war on our rabbits. The soft red pine country was riddled with current and disused rabbit holes where the myxomatosis virus, released some years before, had for a time thinned the population.

If there is a rabbit heaven, the soft soil between the rocks of those hills must have been it. We stuck pieces of rag soaked in fumigant down their burrows, and then collapsed the tunnels. We dug in the disused ones and burnt the surrounding hollow logs. We carefully laid out trails of diced carrots, and after they had acquired the taste, we laced the carrot with poison. The rabbits were always there, but by whittling away at them, we did make a difference.

Standing on the black-soil flat of our highest hill, I could look out over the Western Plains until they were lost in the distant haze. I saw a wonderful sight of yellow wheat paddocks, brown fallow, and soft green, all dotted with those solitary Kurrajongs laid out in miniature. The background behind, and around to the right, was a view of the blue Warrumbungles keeping their watch, and the Spire, where it stood majestic at the head of our valley.

They say you learn as you go, and in the early days, the pony and I learned to scramble up and down the slopes without a slip or a fall. Danny the sheep dog with his mixture of Kelpie and Border Collie was a remarkable animal and, with his lady friend scampering not far behind, would cast out wide. They would go up or down the hills to find the sheep and bring them to me. I like to think that somewhere out there in those hills, their distant offspring are still eagerly running after sheep.

Although I was not conscious of it at the time, nor did he ever discuss it with me, but my father and my mother would have had their differences. Recalling it now, I am not sure she was at all keen on making her life with him on his idyll, his chosen patch of vertical hills. Nonetheless, she kept up a steady flow of correspondence, and made one or two short investigative trips to see what we were up to, before she decided whether or not to join us.

When at last she did, she arrived, closely followed by a couple of house painters from Sydney. They were followed by a team of local plumbers and builders, and much coming and going, and in short order, we had an inside toilet, hot water on tap, bright colors everywhere, curtains on the windows, and carpet on the floor. Suddenly, he and I had been gentrified; the days of living rough and throwing a couple of chops direct on the stove top, or cooking our evening meal over a fire in the living room, were gone forever.

My mother, having made her decision, threw herself with great success into being a country wife. Before I left, she and I planted out the garden with jasmine, roses, and all kinds of shrubs and flowers, including fantastic gladioli. They, provided they had enough water, grew to perfection in the rich soil. We also grew all our own vegetables, which had a wonderful taste and were far superior to any we purchased.

This reunion began another chapter of their lives and they appeared happy together. He took her out along those bumpy tracks we had made to show her what had been done. Off they would go in the cool of early evening, walking or driving up the paddocks to see the cattle or the sheep, or perhaps just to lean over a fence and admire a stand of new lucerne slowly emerging from beneath a crop of wheat. At night, they would sit by the fire to read and listen to music.

Whatever their problems, their new life brought them closer together. As for me, this had been the once-only and life-shaping experience of a son getting to know his father. There had been the satisfaction of working with him on a new and worthwhile venture, which in my eyes had now come to an end. I had purchased a second-hand Peugeot with reclining front bucket seats, transverse springs, overdrive, and a radio. It was fantastic to be young and to own a French car which, in my eyes, possessed such flair.

I suppose there were things he or I could have said, but never did; but as young men do, I had begun to wonder where I might put my roots down, and where all my hard work was leading—the same thoughts as farmers' sons anywhere and, like them, I had acquired all the skills and knowledge that were to be of little use in my future life in the city. But I knew every tree, every rock, every hidden grassy place; I knew them all, and had them stored away in a gallery of my favorite landscapes.

My memory was of changing seasons, the first winter showing of rye, and of patches of the lush flowering clover in spring. There was the sudden growth of paddy melons, which were a bit like Jack's beanstalk, which, after the sharp summer storms, could suddenly appear out of nowhere. There were shivering dawns with the white layer of mist rising from the creeks, and the sight of bald-faced cattle going down to water. The brilliance of those superb moon- and star-lit nights, the endless path of the Milky Way, which was like a heavenly pathway of a million candelabras! There was the wonder and joy of each new crop of wheat, and I had held the plump new grain, which, like all farmers, I felt we had grown with our own bare hands.

The newborn lambs had been shepherded as they first stood in the morning sun, and I had helped their mothers to stand up and had pulled calves from weakened cows. I had witnessed the relentless grip of fierce and uncompromising drought, and felt the hopelessness of yet another blood-red and dust-smeared sunset. On chilled winter nights, we had stoked a hundred fires; and after rain had made savory the smell of newly turned earth, I had known the sublime satisfaction of what we had achieved. I had got to know my father, and we had made something worthwhile out of a clapped out wilderness.

I still retain an endless kaleidoscope of those years, of him drenching sheep, or standing in the fork of a Kurrajong tree above the hungry stock, my mother dressed to attend a meeting of the Country Women's' Association, or of her pottering around in the garden. In my mind's eye are vivid pictures of him in his favorite khaki overalls, bloodied and dusty from marking lambs, or a new drop of calves. I see him in his old grey hat, counting a mob of sheep and singing out the hundreds; there are a thousand wonderful memories.

Call that time with him, and later with her, a sublime chance or a beautiful gift I may easily have missed; for the taciturn man and his wife were killed by a drunken driver just a few years after I had left. They were leaving on a well-earned holiday to visit their daughter and grandchildren. Any death like that is, of course, the most useless waste of life. But I am grateful to have had that time, and to have retained the memories.

Playground Diplomacy

I was never one of those loud, hyperactive children you hear so much about nowadays. But I do remember being a pupil at our local primary school and trying to play marbles in the dust while my class mates and I were being harassed and bullied by a bigger kid. He was the much-feared "Fishhead" Williams, a tough kid with red hair, bare feet, and short pants, who was in a year ahead of me at school. For children of that age, say seven or eight, that single year made a huge difference.

Extraordinary for me, for, on this occasion, I had thrown off my normal fear, and had rushed in and thrown a lucky punch, which had caught Fishhead right in the solar plexus. And much to my amazement, he began to howl, slunk away, and never troubled us again. I suppose that was one of life's early lessons, as before then, there had been much for little boys to fear. But more about Fishhead later. Like most small boys, we played 'Cowboys and Indians', which we had learned about at the local picture theatre on a Saturday afternoon. There we saw Hopalong Cassidy and Tom Mix wiping out an endless supply of Red Indians.

Although I thoroughly enjoyed those tender years, and for a while, I fancied myself as having been a street urchin during the Second World War, largely because I had fond memories of running around Double Bay bare-footed. Our feet got so tough, we never felt the sharp stones or the cold. So much for the fantasy, as I certainly cannot rate myself as having ever been a genuine street urchin. The reality was that while our father was away fighting the war, my brother, sister, and I were always well-clothed and fed. But our mother was a busy lady, who, with some considerable entrepreneurial skill, ran a busy corner grocery shop that were so prevalent in those days before the coming of the supermarket. As children, we enjoyed a great deal of freedom.

We were never very conscious of the adult war, for we had grown up with it, and were kept busy waging a local war of our own. Our gang comprised all the kids, who, like me, mostly lived in the three-story blocks of flats in Stafford Street. Our war was fought against the Pearce Street kids, who lived just around the corner. I am not sure how this gang warfare started, perhaps to mimic the real one that had taken our fathers away. Their street had been named after Bobby Pearce, Australia's world-famous rower, and the family had well-known sporting identities.

Although we were kids, the gangs had rules, even if, at times, they were obscure. The word would go out where and when a battle was to be fought, although mostly it was fought at the corner of those two streets. We used metal garbage bin lids as our shields, and threw chunks of crushed blue metal at each other that we had pinched from a dump of road-base kept in the nearby municipal works compound. They were just the right size for throwing and were known to us as 'gibbers'. When the battle began, there was much taunting and yelling at the enemy, running up and hurling a gibber at them, and then retreating. Yet, in all the battles that raged, I cannot recall that anyone was ever hurt.

The fear of being unexpectedly ambushed was a constant threat, although an informal truce was in place for going to and from school, or when playing cricket or footy down in the local park. But going through their territory, or for them to pass through ours, could be a cause for battle. For instance, the quickest way to the local swimming pool was through their territory. For little kids, this was quite a problem in the summer months, which caused us many a long, hot detour. But, for them to get to the local park to play cricket or kick a football, they had to pass through our territory.

There were also long periods during which our war was forgotten, and we went fishing, rode our bicycles, and did the myriad of other things little kids do. We could stand on the beach and throw pebbles and watch them skip across the water. Everyone climbed the big rock on the shore by the storm water channel, or got a cardboard carton from the back of mum's shop, and used it to slide down the grass hill at the top of Williams St. And the very low tides of summer enabled us to go wading out on the mud bank, to experience the delicious squelch of mud between our toes and to spear a crab or an octopus.

Three or four times a week, we could stand on the shore and would watch an old fisherman named Joe and his offsider, a retarded man called Bob. As the tide was coming in, they would set a long fishing net over the mud bank, letting it out over the stern of their rowing boat. Then at full tide, they would stand on the beach and haul in the catch. The fish went into empty kerosene tins and this ritual went on, summer and winter. Then their launch would putter across the harbor to the Zoo, where the catch was fed to the animals.

At that age, little boys like to run free, and after school, we went swimming at Red Leaf Pool, which was just a fenced-off slice of the harbor to make it shark-proof. Or we played football or cricket in the park. Anyone could join in, and it didn't matter how many there were on either side. Sometimes we pretended we were long-distance runners and just ran around and around the park.

George was a young man, who probably for some unknown medical reason, had escaped military service and worked for my mother in her shop. He also used a lot of hair oil, as he had cultivated a spectacular cowlick, which hung just over his forehead. George was good at what he did, made magnificent displays of cans of food and bottles of drink, and served behind the counter. He looms large in my memory as he encouraged my football and gave me his old football boots. They were miles too big, but I did not mind a bit, as it was explained to me that I would grow into them. Meanwhile, I wore three pairs of socks, and packed the toes with newspaper.

Toward the end of the war, some new kids came to our school and became known to us as "reffos", and they introduced us to a round ball and a game we came to know as soccer. I vividly remember one of the first, a voluble French kid named Raymond Prevot, who, although he struggled with his English, would expressively use his hands to make himself understood. During a game, he would run up to the ball and really slam it. Raymond was our first introduction to the flood of displaced persons who were to settle in Australia after the Second World War.

One of my heroes was a teenager known as "Ocka" Kelly, who never wore shoes and would often be down the park to kick a football around. He could set the ball on the ground and kick it further and higher with the ball of his foot than most kids, even if they were wearing footy boots.

When the American servicemen were on leave in Sydney, they often hired motorboats from Messenger's Boatshed and took their girlfriends out for a day on the harbor. And, not being aware of the local hazards, such as the mud bank, which ran out parallel to the wharf and was often covered with just a few inches of water. The kids waited for them to run aground, at which there would be a mad rush to wade out and push them free, as during the shortages of wartime, they were our only source of chewing gum and Coca-Cola.

But I was telling you about this bully known as "Fishhead" Williams, and how he had us little kids bluffed. It got serious when he punched one of my friends on the nose and made it bleed. Fishhead lived somewhere beyond the shopping center and had attached himself to the Pearce St Gang. It was rumored that he would bash us up if he ever caught us on our own.

Now my mother's corner shop was just up the road from our primary school, and on a winter day, I could go there and Mrs. French, who made up the school lunches, would make me something hot for my lunch. I could have a tin of baked beans or something like that, which I would eat straight out of a green enamel saucepan. I was told to keep out of sight of the customers, and to eat my lunch sitting on a butter box behind the stainless-steel fridge.

But you know how it is when you're a kid, and when no one was looking, I used to gaze at the display of confectionary and fantasize about eating a stick of licorice or a chocolate frog. And there was always the chance the cabinet may have been left open, and if no one was looking, I could pinch something. But not on this occasion, for who should I see staring at the array of sweets from the other side of the glass case? It was none other than the fearsome mug of Fishhead Williams. He glared a menacing scowl when he saw me, crossed his eyes, and poked his tongue out.

I was trapped, and was likely to be bashed up on way back to school. And worse, he had now discovered where I sometimes had lunch. And just as I was contemplating all this, the ample figure of Mrs. French appeared around the corner of the fridge to see how I was getting on. In a flash of sheer brilliance, I said to her, "Mrs. French, do you think Fishhead Williams from our school could have a rainbow ball or a musk stick?"

"Goodness me, haven't you grown!" she said, to my antagonist on other side of the counter. "You're Beryl William's little boy, aren't you? Say hello to your mother for me, and tell her I don't know how she copes with your father being overseas."

Then, after a brief pause, she said to me, "Now ask your friend if he would like an ice cream, and I don't think your mother would mind if you each had a chocolate frog to take back to school."

"Yeah, he would," I said, "but not for me. Thanks Mrs. French, 'cause I don't feel well."

"I'll have his," said Fishhead, "'cause him and me are best friends."

Part II - Young Adulthood

Hindsight is a Beautiful Thing

When Robert Gordon Menzies was the Prime Minister of Australia, he brought in a military training program for eighteen-year-old men known as "The National Service Training Scheme". Our intake went into camp as the Nineteenth National Service Training Battalion at Holdsworthy Army Barracks, which was about an hour's train ride out of Sydney. At school, I had been a keen member of the Military Cadet Corps and knew my left foot from my right, how to clean, strip, and fire a Bren gun, a Lee Enfield rifle, and I was also proficient in the Vickers machine gun, which I think explains how, after a few weeks of camp, I was chosen to attend a potential officers training course; although, the title of this course was much grander than the reality.

The Army in those days had a very a masochistic approach to running such courses, for they maintained a policy of making things as miserable as possible for the young men attending them. This would have been, presumably, in the hope that at the end, to the candidate at any rate, their wounding, and/or death in battle, would not seem such a bad outcome. The day began early in the morning with a parade in full kit, the presentation of which had to be pristine. That was the theory, but as a part of the regime, they embraced, it never was, and never could be. So our packs and webbing were endlessly cleaned, our boots shone like they were lacquered, and endless hours were spent polishing our brass. Thus, when they had reduced our resistance and our brains to the consistency of chicken mash, and we had lost the power of individual thought, in their eyes, we were ready to go forward.

After that course, I firmly believe you can brainwash any group of eighteen-year-olds so that they accept absolutely anything. Having been told that we were the cream of Australian manhood and how very clever we were, we were silly enough to start to believe it. They trained us to within an inch of our lives, and it was put to us that our excelling in close order drill had prepared us for all that life or battle could throw in our paths. How naive we were, not that we had any option other than to agree!

We could stand dead still like the Grenadier Guardsmen outside the Buckingham Palace, and into whose impassive faces passing tourists poke their cameras. Who would not want to go out and die for Queen and country after a day or so of doing that? Our instructors were overweight warrant officers, whom, we found, were the real engine that ran the army, those of superior officer rank simply being there for obscure and ancient ceremonial purposes.

The WO's filled the days and nights with drill, exercises, and lectures on all kinds of military topics, but basically they had us picturing marauding hordes arriving on our shores, intent on performing much killing, rape, and plundering as they ran amok across our country. They had us running about at night with fixed bayonets while we practiced the shooting, the smashing of skulls, and much stabbing and slashing the enemy.

After a few weeks of this, we had reached a pitch, so that charging the enemy with fixed bayonets would have seemed like a glorious release. They paraded us at the end of our course so the Colonel could make a long-winded speech about nothing that had any relevance to anything we had done; and then they set us free. We were presented with our Lance Corporal's stripes and turned loose to train our fellow National Servicemen on how to fight a war.

Or that was what the army hoped.

My father had been very keen on all this, as he had been in the Second World War; so at least I had a smattering of what the Army was about. However, there was one vital ingredient missing, which made his war very different from our time in uniform. And no matter what way you looked at it, it made it very difficult to pretend it was there, for we had no enemy, and as a consequence, it was very hard to conjure up a war, or for that matter, even the threat of one. So there was a general feeling among the recruits that being called up was nothing but a waste of our time, not to mention the loss of income, and was an unwelcome intrusion into our lives. This state of affairs did not dawn on me, as it should have, and my awakening arrived with all the subtlety of being run over by a Bondi bus.

Indeed, it was a strange experience for a cross section of eighteen-year-old men to be thrown together like that. Off parade, we all got on famously; and if the occasion, such as a birthday, warranted it, we might even get drunk together; although, until we settled down, one or two recruits liked to think they were tougher than they actually were. The favored card game was Five Hundred, which went on by torchlight after lights out, or any time we weren't doing anything. I would say that, for the bulk of the recruits, and with the lack of an enemy, and long days of incessant drill and marching about, their time there would have passed very slowly.

We had a Pooh-faced Englishman, a particularly vicious-minded regular army type, as our Platoon Sergeant. This fiend had stormed ashore at Normandy during the Second World War, or so he said. Our view was that it was very bad luck that this obnoxious man had survived, and had had himself transferred out of the British Army to carry on his war, and to make our lives a misery.

However, the unwelcome presence of this tortured soul was offset by a regular army corporal, who had been to the Korean War, and was a fine leader of men and much liked. Our Commanding Officer was a pale-faced Second Lieutenant, a graduate of the Portsea Military College, who minced about in a very unconvincing manner. Who, as far as anyone could determine, given the Sergeant ran us, like a mad African tyrant, had absolutely nothing to do all day. Thus he kept up a pretence that he was attending to the weighty matters of command.

My course at the Potential Officers Training School had finished; so it was that I found myself newly promoted, and wearing one solitary stripe on each arm. Thus, I confidently marched my new command out through the barrack gates. This "command" comprised one Section of about a dozen men, whom I marched down the road until I found a suitably shaded patch, where I could deliver my introductory lesson on the Bren gun. Along we went—me with my head held high, shoulders back, arms swinging as I marched along and singing out the time, "left right, left right." As they marched, my Section would have occasionally been admonished with, "no talking in the ranks, eyes to the front, left right, left right." When we arrived, I had them gather around, so I could deliver the lesson.

I would have opened the way I had been taught by the overweight but zealous warrant officers, with a statement designed to command respect and interest.

"Today, men, we are going to learn about the Bren gun. We will learn all the skills that will make you effective with this basic infantry weapon. What you learn may even save your life, and those of your mates, should we have to go to war."

Very profound and telling words, I would have thought. I could see that Private Fred Woods was picking his nose and looking at me in a most peculiar fashion. Fred lived with his widowed mother in a tiny flat near the beach at Bondi, and told the most incredible and, to me, shocking stories. They were about picking up "sheilas", getting drunk for days at a time, and bashing up other blokes he did not like in the local pub.

Then I noticed "Frosty" Jones, who had his hands in his pockets, and his eyes averted heavenwards as if he was waiting for divine intervention. Now, as it happened, most of these fellows were old friends, who knocked about together in civilian life. They went to the same surf club dances, and led lives rich in surfing culture. This, according to them, was overflowing with alcohol and much free-wheeling fornication.

I had got about as far as demonstrating how the weapon could be stripped down, and explaining how it operated, when I noticed "Spud" Mulligan was looking at me in his odd sideways manner. Private Mulligan had a scar from his ear to near the base of his nose, from a fight he claimed he had won. This was in a time before the advent of cheap Asian imports. Mulligan was well-known as a low-cost source of watches, radios, and other expensive merchandise. How he came by them is probably best left unexplained.

Then he said in his particular "don't mess with me" tone of his, "Listen Corp, there is no bloody war going on, and we don't want to stand around like a lot of flaming galahs listening to you carrying on all day." This announcement produced a few "bloody oaths" and "yeahs" from some of his mates. There was an awkward silence. Then one of them, Private Woods, continued the mood with, "otherwise mate, we might just be forced to... you bloody well know." There was no mistaking the threat.

There are times when my brain races ahead and thinks faster than it normally does. This was one of those occasions. Maintaining command, as taught, and gathering myself to my full height of five feet and ten inches, I sang out my well-considered next command.

"Those of you who will not pay attention and wish to be a party to this threat may fall out over there and play Five Hundred. But you should understand that if the Sergeant comes along, you will be clapped in the brig and charged with insubordination and threatening a non-commissioned officer."

No one moved. Years later, the thought occurred to me that just maybe our English Sergeant had good reason for his uncompromising bastardry, and that perhaps my course had taught me something useful after all.

Acceptable Dress

There was a time when I had a very nice English girlfriend. You may have read, or if you were old enough, may even remember when the Liberal government of Australia's Prime Minister Bob Menzies was very keen to encourage the British to settle in this faraway land. To entice them, they were offered the highly subsidized fare of ten pounds. The result of this was that thousands of young people, disparagingly labeled "ten pound Poms", suddenly lobbed on our shores. My English girlfriend, a speech therapist from London, was one of them.

I liked them and thought they were more sophisticated than Sydney-siders, adept at conversation and socializing generally. Perhaps it was a lifestyle thing, the result of short days, the pub lifestyle and living in their cold climate. And one Friday night, she and I met after work in the city for a drink at Sydney's latest international hotel. She was wearing a very nice 'pantsuit', which was the latest fashion. No sooner had we ordered a drink, than we were approached, presumably by a headwaiter.

"Sir and Madam, I am very sorry," he announced, "but I have to inform you that women are not allowed to wear pants in the main lounges and dining areas."

Astounded by this ridiculous ruling, and not wishing to embarrass her any further, we got up and left. Slightly miffed at the stupidity of it, we repaired to the more relaxed atmosphere of a hotel down the road, and carried on with our evening. It pleases me that over the years, Sydney has changed very much for the better to become a sophisticated cosmopolitan city, and not before time.

Some years later, my wife and I wanted to mark an occasion by going to an up-market restaurant for dinner. It was a typical humid summer night, and I had not worn a tie. I was studying the menu when a waiter appeared at my side and bent down to my ear to ask confidentially, "Would sir care to borrow this tie for the evening?"

Now, this insistence on dress code was not my style at all, and I was all for us getting up and leaving. Then it occurred to me that perhaps I should bend a little on this occasion. I had married a conservative Adelaide girl, and if draping the offered tie around my neck would please her, then so be it. I am actually fond of Adelaide, although I consider it to be an outpost of English conservatism, which also carries with it the veneer of their class system.

But this hang-up with dress codes, particularly ties, had no end to it, and I am convinced a tourist arriving in Sydney in the middle of summer, and seeing the number of males wearing a collar and tie with a European suit, would have thought us quite mad. After all, they would know that our forebears have been living here for over two hundred years, and had still not adapted to the climate. Perhaps, we are just an outpost of England after all, where ties are worn as a badge of superiority.

I used to be a Sydney real estate agent with a conservative company, and stinking hot, and wringing wet with humidity, or not, my employer insisted we wore a collar and tie, preferably with a suit. If I was envious of anyone, it would have been of many of our clients, who were smart young men who would have not been seen dead wearing a tie.

I once met my brother, a rising city solicitor, in the marble bar of the former 'Ushers Hotel. When the original hotel was demolished, its famous marble bar was reinstalled in the basement of a new hotel. I recall that it was after work on a late Saturday afternoon, and that we had arrived coat-less and tie-less to see the famous old bar in its new home, and to enjoy a convivial drink. And a very nice place it was too, with piped music and air-conditioning, and where attentive staff stood around wearing white shirts and black bow ties. We were happily having a beer and chatting away, when we were approached by one of the staff. Polite as he may have been, we were told we could not drink there unless we were wearing a tie or a cravat.

My brother and I looked at each other in amazement. I was ready to move on, but I could see that he was not going to accept the situation.

With that, he took off a sock and wrapped it around his neck, tucking it under his shirt as a cravat. I followed suit. Then we ordered another beer and continued our conversation.

Saving the Drinks for Later

I am the younger of two brothers, and for those who are not, or worse, do not even have a brother, I had better explain. It is like having a close friend with whom you are constantly at war; that is about all anyone can say about it, and I can't put it any better than that. They are useful for borrowing money, as long as you are doing the borrowing. Well yes, and taking the blame for the bad things you did when you were children at home. Throughout your life, they are also a useful measure as to where you rate in the whole scheme of things. However, I am also willing to vouch that if they own a sailing boat, they can occasionally be thought of as very useful indeed.

My brother and I travelled different paths. As a young man, he was a studious chap heading for a career in) law. For myself, I had a hankering for the country life and I headed for the bush, which I enjoyed very much. One of the things I got from my young country friends was their genuine inclusiveness, which ensured you were never left out of the orbit of their friendship. Of course, they paired off, but as a group, it was nothing to spend the weekend together, playing tennis, often staying with someone who lived in town. Saturday night, we would most probably go to the same party, and that's only a distant snapshot of it.

Career opportunities were very limited for young people in country towns, and I understand they still are. So one by one, they would drift away to the city: the girls to go nursing, attend university or a business school; the boys to get a degree, become builders, teachers, and surveyors, and so on. But the nice thing was that we kept in touch. I had met Kelly and Joanna through the tennis club, where we had played most weekends in the small country town of Coonabarabran.

This was one of those drive-through country towns, a place you briefly see on the way to somewhere else. When I knew it, the highway went right through the middle of the town and also served as the main street. The cars parked angled to the curb, and there was a row of shops on either side, and that was about it. I should mention the turkey farm, the renowned radio telescope, the railway station, the airport, and the golf, tennis, and bowling clubs.

This small town lies in the middle of the Warrumbungle Mountains, although you would hardly call them 'mountains' in the European alpine sense. They are really the remnants of a range of ancient volcanoes, where many rock cores can still be seen. The eroded soil from them is the source of the rich farmlands on the slopes and plains that surround them.

This story took place in a year when, after the hard work of putting in a wheat crop, I came down to Sydney for a break. It was the middle of winter, and Kelly was in her first or second year of nursing, while Joanna worked in a Judge's chamber. I am sure you recall how young people like to brag, and I was no exception. I had often mentioned that my brother owned a sailing boat, and what terrific fun it was skimming around Sydney Harbor. In these situations, there comes a time when you have to deliver, which explains why I had asked them out for a day's sailing. And I am still in my brother's debt over what happened.

The chosen day was cold and overcast, and a general storm warning had been issued for a southerly buster to arrive later in the day. This I had studiously taken care not to mention. The girls and I went to my brother's flat, where we changed into our sailing gear. I look back upon it with a genuine feeling of guilt, for against his better judgment, I had browbeaten him into taking us out.

There was one thing he and I always agreed on, and that was the need for good food and drink; and we catered very well. Among other things, we had nicely made sandwiches in a waterproof hamper. Also, as it was the middle of winter, and just before we set off from the shore, I gave a bottle of brandy to Kelly to mind; and I thought the occasion called for a bottle of champagne, which I gave to Joanna.

My brother was and still is a pretty good skipper, and we began with a rip-roaring ride across the water to Athol Bay, and the girls loved it. We were all leaning over the side to counter the wind, the boat bouncing across the waves and spray flying everywhere. Then we made a broad reach down past Shark Island, and then we went about and fairly flew back again.

We made a very comfortable leg just off Kirribilli, which gave the girls a great view of the Sydney Opera House. I think the harbor is a wonderful escape from the mad bustle of the city. Bouncing across the waves and scudding back to Rose Bay, the wind was getting a little colder; not that anyone minded. Kelly and Joanna were athletic girls, who played good tennis and were also strong swimmers. They were also attractive and gregarious, and like most country girls, who helped on the farm, they could turn their hand to most things. Kelly had long auburn hair, which she had wrapped in a scarf, and Joanna kept telling us what a fantastic time she was having.

As sailors know, there is a very strange phenomenon that can happen once a skipper steps on board their yacht, which I can best liken to a chameleon hopping from one bush to another, and changing their color. For instance, I once sailed on a racing yacht, where the skipper was a perfectly charming fellow on dry land, but turned into a raging tyrant once he was on board. And I am not even sure you can pick it. Oh yes, and I recall a skipper, who during the week, was a powerful executive of a major company in the city. But once he stepped on board his yacht, he completely changed into someone akin to a neurotic housewife, and would fuss around and begin wiping everything down with a soft cloth. I mean it was bad: if you were offered a drink you dreaded to put it down in case you marked the polished wood. He actually reminded me of my dear mother, who had the annoying habit of puffing up the lounge chair cushions as soon as anyone got up.

I was saying that my brother was a very competent skipper, and as I look back, it is difficult to differentiate between our ongoing war and any personality changes he may have gone through once he stepped on board. And I have to say that on this day, he was charm itself. I also think he was very taken with our delightful guests. But I can recall that if he was racing, he could make things pretty tense for the crew.

He was always very conscious of safety, and I admire the fact that he had carefully packed floatation under the deck. That is the white lightweight Styrofoam packaging that comes with new electrical goods, and which you can never get rid of. This meant that in the event of a capsize, his boat was unsinkable.

I should at least explain that a 'reach' is when the wind is coming in from the side, and that it is a fast and exhilarating point of sailing. That day, we reached back and forth between Shark Island, which is in the middle of Rose Bay, and Clarke Island, which ferry travelers will know is just off the tip of Darling Point. The girls had been terrific friends of mine, and I got a great kick out of organizing a day out on the harbor. They were having a wonderful time, and my brother was excelling himself. I nursed the champagne while Joanna took a turn at the tiller, and we flew across the water; then he gave Kelly a steer, while I looked after the brandy.

Meanwhile, big black thunderheads were gathering in the south.

Clearly, my brother was getting all the glory. I mean the girls knew I could hit a tennis ball, ride a horse, and sink a tankard of beer as quick as anyone. They also knew I was handy on the dance floor, and not too bad around a snooker table.

When it was my turn to take the tiller, he gave me that look that clearly said, "If you break anything, or tip us over, I will personally slowly strangle you to death with my own bare hands." The message was unmistakable, but with the tiller in my hand, all my boyhood sailing skills came flooding back.

"Pull the main and jib on," I ordered as I lined up the forestay with the Convent on the distant slope of Vaucluse.

"Ready, coming about, lee oh," I called with the devil-may-care air of a seasoned salt, as I swung the boat around.

Our lunch was to be at Seven Shillings Beach, which, on most days, would be sheltered from the wind, and I was thinking about heading that way. But as we sailed a little way off Point Piper, it had started to rain, which tends to calm the water in a blow, so at times it was almost still, except for the splash of rain. After ripping across the bay in an exhilarating dash, we would have been no more than fifty yards from the rocky shore of Darling Point, when a blast of violent cold air hit us unexpectedly from the south. I think it must have been deflected by the eastern shore of the point.

It was all over in an instant, although the tip of the mast hovered for a few seconds just above the water, before another gust knocked us flat. The girls came up spluttering, but were able to laugh at our situation. Knowing the drill, I swam out to support the tip of the mast so the boat could not roll right over. I worried about the much dreaded loss or breakage of gear. We were quite safe, the girls treading water and hanging on to the boat, and our skipper, as calm as you like, was securing everything.

Meanwhile, the rain had stopped and the wind was piping in at around thirty-five knots from the south, and roughing up the water. Driven by wind and waves, we were slowly being carried toward the end of the point. On the shore, a few onlookers were anxiously waving us in, while others watched this little drama from their balconies.

Not far away, there was a private beach, and, worried the girls were getting cold, it was decided I should swim them in, leaving my brother with the boat. Their faces, whether it was the cold, the shock, or both, were very pale; but staying together, we slowly made it to shore. By that time a man with a dingy had attached a line to the bow.

Meanwhile, we huddled together on the beach, trying to keep out of the wind, and watched as the boat was towed in. I felt guilty and mightily embarrassed by all this, but the girls were in good spirits and perhaps they thought this sort of thing was usual.

"That was terrific fun," said the pale and bedraggled Kelly, producing her bottle of brandy and laying it on the sand.

"It was," said Joanna, "I would not have missed it for anything." With that, she triumphantly produced the bottle of champagne, "At least we have been able to save the drinks for later," she said proudly.

Mutual Friends

This is such a bizarre tale that should they come across it now, I doubt that those involved could avoid self-recognition. This story began in an ordinary way. I was a young, enthusiastic, and hard-working real estate salesman, who was hopefully establishing a reputation for selling quality houses and apartments on the north shore of Sydney Harbor. I enjoyed the life; I was gregarious, and to me, it was a pleasure getting to know our vendors, and of course, later on, our buyers. And it also enabled me to meet some well-known people, such as politicians, industrialists, jurists, entertainers, and so on.

Indeed, I met some wonderful people, and I especially enjoyed meeting personalities from the entertainment industry. One of my favorites was the famous ballet dancer and choreographer, Sir Robert Helpman. He was a very charming and quick-witted man, who continually played up to his audience, and he went out of his way to entertain a small group of real estate salespeople, who had combined forces so he could inspect a decent range of quality homes. Sir Robert kept us, and his own retinue, in stitches for the day as we flitted in and out of some of Sydney's finest homes, which were scattered around the harbor side.

Some of our vendors overreacted when they found out who was coming, and I can recall one society matron meeting us in full evening dress at ten in the morning. There were a lot of homes to see, and we were much amused as the famous star's quips passed right over an owner's head, as the ballet star literally danced in and out of their homes. The price of which may have just dramatically risen to match the fame of the buyer.

I once had the pleasure of squiring an exquisite Afro-American Hollywood star, who had a delightful personality to match. She was sick to death of being hounded by the media and of being stuck in hotels. So just for a joke, and she was great fun to be with, I took this delightful creature through a home where I knew my wife was attending a ladies' bridge day. The bridge tournament was stopped dead in its tracks when the star swept in, and I know she and the players enjoyed her visit immensely. I only mention her and my day with Sir Robert to illustrate that the industry does have some high notes.

I was trying to build up my personal goodwill, which worked like this: I would receive a referral from a client, a friend or a solicitor and, as a result, I would have another decent home for sale.

Now this tale involves an affable lady in her later middle years who had been a widow for some time. But, unfortunately for her, the Sydney housing market was going through one of its cyclical phases and was barely turning over at all; believe me it was so flat that, as a man with a family, I worked seven days a week in a battle to keep afloat.

At that time, I had been showing a very charming young woman through as many houses as I could, as I was convinced she was ready to buy. And it was no onerous task to chat with her as we drove around from one house to the next. I had not yet met her husband, but I knew from our conversations that he was one of the Livingston-Wadderspoons, a wealthy polo-playing family with a string of vast pastoral properties stretching up through New South Wales and Queensland.

I think you can imagine what happened when Gloria Livingston-Wadderspoon and I arrived at the home. For as soon as they were introduced, the owner immediately recognized Gloria's surname, and from that moment, gushed over us; and that included the offer of afternoon tea. I then arranged to show Gloria and her husband through the home together. But, for some forgotten reason, the appointment was put off until the following Sunday. The husband turned out to be a pleasant man, but for this inspection, the vendor had prepared with a vengeance; and the tea things stood ready, including scones and two varieties of cake. I am sure my owner was already counting the proceeds of the sale of her home, and I was confident that I was going to put it together.

However, sometimes these things are not meant to be, and at the time, I thought I must have misread the young couple's intentions, as they appeared to have gone cold on that home. So you can imagine my surprise when some months later, I saw their car in the driveway; and when I checked, I found a sale to the Livingston-Wadderspoons had taken place.

But as they say, "you can't win them all," and I had long recognized that an essential requirement for a sale is the honesty of all those involved. If it isn't there, and a misrepresentation is made, or somebody does the wrong thing, apart from legal action, there is not a lot you can do about it. Similarly, if it is the agent who is cut out, there is not much he or she can do without entering an uncertain legal fight. After the disappointment, it seemed to me that the smart thing was to move on, and in time, I forgot about my avaricious owner and her opportunistic buyers.

Ah, but the world can be a small place, and when I first came to Sydney, I had met a very charming young couple who had also just arrived, and we became lifelong friends. We had arrived eager to find fame and fortune. I was still single and had a tedious job in the city. As the years rolled on, they had their children and prospered, as eventually my wife and I did; and we would have watched each other's progress through life with some satisfaction.

The husband was a notable businessman and a gregarious net worker; and one day, he called to ask if my wife and I would attend a luncheon at which there would be political leaders and all the top people from the finance and property industries. This, he assured me, was an occasion I should not miss. And believe me, it was an impressive affair, black-jacketed waiters plied us with drinks and delicious things to nibble, as we were introduced and circulated around.

Before long, it was announced that lunch was to be served, and we were ushered into the dining room. A seating plan told us where to sit: my wife was to be on the other side of the person on my right, a Mr. Livingston-Wadderspoon; it could not be the same, but it was; and on my left was none other than the charming Gloria Livingston-Wadderspoon.

You may wonder how I handled this; perhaps it was a personal failing; but I chose to do nothing, absolutely nothing. With Gloria, there had been a few initial telltale flushes and her husband avoided anything but the barest of perfunctory conversations one might have with a perfect stranger. There was no hint of recognition and he began a conversation with my wife, whereas Gloria and I, and it was she who brought the subject up, pretended that apart from her vague remembrance of us meeting during her search for a home, we were perfect strangers, and we proceeded to carry on a conversation about horses.

About this time, my friend came up and, clapping the husband and me on the shoulders, commented, "I just knew you two guys would get on like a house on fire," and after much good-humored banter of the sort designed to bind mutual friends, left to continue his meeting and greeting.

But an hour or so of good food and the imbibing of fine wine broke down the barriers of restraint, for in a complete turnabout, Gloria suddenly lent across.

"Darling," she directed at her husband, "you must remember Geoffrey; he was that very obliging real estate man we met when we were searching for a home."

I was content to let her remark go by and for them to play it any way they wished.

"Really?" he said, with pretended astonishment.

I had drawn my chair back a little way from the table in the hope that my wife could join in the conversation. The husband did likewise, so we formed our own little circle. But my wife was more aware than I knew. She looked at them and smiled, as if she was remembering something from the distant past. Then she said, "My husband would have remembered; he always does; he is from the country you know; and I believe what shocked him about your behavior was knowing you were from such an illustrious pastoral family."

That faint smile had lingered as she spoke, while the faces of Gloria and her husband had lit up like the crimson glow of a glorious bush sunset.

I Just Adore Banking

I have a phobia that I struggle with, and that is a deep fear of banks. This was not helped when I recently read in the financial papers of the huge losses, measured in billions, incurred by my own bank. Considering that a billion dollars is a thousand million, the amount of the bank's loss was staggering.

Just reading about it took me back to a time when we were young, and my wife and I were buying our first home. If you have been through that yourself, you will remember. Even finding the home you want to live in, and then entering into the awe-inspiring lifelong debt, is a trial in itself. But like everyone else, we did, and negotiated to buy our home from a very nice couple.

They had a dear little boy and a Dalmatian, and begged us to come back on a summer evening, which we did, and during which they plied us with sherry and much charm, to which we succumbed. They also included the refrigerator, and a few other handy things we lacked, as added inducements.

We paid a ten percent deposit and engaged a lawyer, "a piece of cake," you might say, for we had twenty-five years in which to pay off the whopping debt. However, before we could move in, we had to wait for our bank to pay the charming couple the other ninety percent of the purchase price.

So where's the problem? The house would be ours on the following Friday, or so our lawyer assured us. But, purely as a courtesy, I phoned our friendly bank manager to remind him that Friday was the big day. What on earth was this? A peculiar vagueness had descended over our housing transaction; "this Friday?" he queried, as if I had just suggested something outrageous.

On my end of the phone, I was breaking out in a terrible sweat. I did follow what was happening in the world, and I could sense what was coming, and I think you know when people are deliberately avoiding the issue. A lot of throat clearing, coughing, and spluttering was coming to me over the line. "Unfortunately," he said, "our bank can no longer see its way clear to fund the purchase of this home as there has been a change in our lending policy."

Had I heard him right? This was one hell of a jam to be in, which is to be polite about it! I should explain that the economies of the western world were in a mess; the price of crude oil had gone through the roof; the share market had collapsed; and our and everyone else's situation in suburban Australia was grim. My wife and I owed the charming couple ninety percent of the purchase price of their home. They were buying elsewhere, and I was sure would sue us for every cent we had, or would ever earn in our lives; and of course, our ten percent deposit would be gone forever.

Thoroughly crushed, and numbed in a state of shock, I got on the train and went into the city, and propelled myself into the state head office of the bank. I was distressed and demanded to see the General Manager, and was left waiting in a vast, hushed, marble executive reception area. How lucky I was, for he was charm itself, as he made a phone call and assured me that our loan was in place, which made me wonder what would have been the fate of anyone in the same position, who did not go in and make a fuss? In great relief, I went into the nearest bar and downed a neat brandy.

A nice conclusion—the garden flourished, our babies arrived, and our lives continued on their merry way. I should mention that our bank held personal guarantees from my wife and me, and of course, the first mortgage on our home. So they were well and truly covered.

That period of your life can hold many rewards for a young couple. As part of the community, you meet other parents and make new friends. They include your neighbors, who can be a bit up and down, as everyone soon discovers. Ours were pretty good, but we did have our moments. There was the obligatory older couple who said they knew my family, a vague threat of retribution, if ever there was one. And yet, one day I received a phone call from the husband to pop in on my way home. Could this really be the "getting to know the new neighbor's crackers and cheese, served with a cold beer?" Never; it was for him to inform me that the roots of our trees were slowly boring into the pipes of their lovely home; actually it wasn't, and was as nondescript as its owners. Nevertheless, they insisted that our roots were causing incredible havoc, given with the reminder that they knew my family. You can see the connection: pay for the repairs or else...

There had been one neighboring couple, who, when they moved in, were so shy that they would not even acknowledge our cat, one of those big, friendly, ginger ones that came with the house and made a point of rubbing against a visitor's leg. But children again; and in no time, theirs were in and out, soon to be followed by the mother and father, who, as the relationship progressed, were more in our place than out of it. There was another neighbors—the perennial handyman, forever drilling and grinding—a hobbyist whose boat-building glues stank to high heaven whenever the wind blew from his direction.

But generally, everyone got on famously, and it was wonderful the range of people you met, only to find they lived just up the road. There was one couple in particular, and our friendship started very gingerly, a holding back as if there might be some reason why it should not progress, which had left us wondering.

But as I said, what with children, local school fund-raising events, and Christmas parties, any reticence soon evaporated. The other young parents knew about the ups and downs of living in suburbia. The husband was a banker, and, within his orbit, knew a few things about me, which I did not know myself. Hence the reserve. But over a drink, he revealed the incredible fact that I was on a little-known bankers' black list. This, in bankers' speak, meant that except for the existing housing loan, I was done for—an "untouchable" in any lender's eyes.

This explained why my bank manager had given me the cold shoulder. But the rub was that this was a highly illegal act for any bank to engage in, and in doing so, they would have broken every privacy law in the land. The obvious reason was that a few years before, I had been caught out with some small investment property. The real estate market had suddenly collapsed, leaving me stranded, and it had taken me some time to sell the property and clear my debt. But unknown to me, the damage had already been done.

Finding out about that black list had led me to again approach the bank, and to the setting up of my own business. This was the moment when instinct told me it was time to stand up and slay a dragon; as I never thought we were designed to stay in one place like an old tree stump. With this approach, I had dropped the clanger that I thought I might be on their secret blacklist, which was like telling the Chairman of the Board that if he did not come across, my good friend, the President of the United States, would lob a missile right through their boardroom window.

The shock and horror of that led to an interview at the head office, a ride around the city in a plush limousine, and a more senior manager of a bigger branch being charged with looking after the affairs of their, suddenly, "very important and most valuable customer".

Meanwhile, the years rolled by, and we found it fascinating to watch our own and the neighborhood children go through school and slowly grow up. It was quite competitive, and we saw how other parents got on, the husbands often maturing into high-profile figures in commerce and industry. Others went into politics, ran shops, built factories, or became artists or writers. Some worked faithfully for businesses which suddenly collapsed; and we celebrated when they got another job, and prospered again. For others, sickness or accident happened, and every now and then, couples fell in or out of love, and moved on to start anew.

Suddenly, there was another world financial crisis and the housing market faltered. I had borrowed as interest rates had shot up and my income had fallen away. As I struggled with the loan, the bank seemed unsure of what to do with the relationship; except, every now and again, they made little sallies during which they would release some money into our account, provided we signed another document that guaranteed their prosperity, come what may.

Then they came up with the delightful tactic of calling me in to discuss the situation. They would say the regular manager was unavailable, and his replacement would be a very uncompromising stranger, who represented the bank's darker side.

Then, there was the famous time when I hit upon the plan of getting close to my bank manager by taking him and his wife out for dinner. The other guests were two close friends of ours—the husband, a successful and very pleasant young man, and his wife, who was a very attractive woman. They would enliven the occasion, as would, of course, my lovely wife.

The format was to have pre-dinner drinks at a smart little bar. The conversation flowed, and there was much laughter and goodwill. Our table was in a pleasant corner and soon the manager's wife was engrossed in conversation with our male friend. Our lady friend was also doing her best to impress the bank manager. She was soon telling him how lucky his bank was to have us as clients.

The bank manager's gaze had not shifted from our glamorous lady friend, particularly her cleavage, which was considerable, and she was playing up to it for all she was worth. This included pouting and chucking him under the chin and, in a very husky voice, whispering, "You know darling, I just adore banking". Even my wife, a woman of liberal views, visibly blanched at this while across the table, my friend and the manager's wife looked as though they were ready to book into a hotel for the night.

After what had been a most convivial meal, we managed to sort ourselves into our taxis and get ourselves home, and for a while, the fallout from that evening worked a treat. The bank manager kept out of my hair, or did until, like all smart new managers, he was drawn up into the inner workings of his bank.

Perhaps, my phobia of banks is overdone, but I heard the other day that their computer had granted a nine-year-old schoolboy a huge line of credit, as it did a client who had been dead for years. These days, I accept that I am just a long sequence of digital numbers, which, wherever I am, tells the bank's computer everything it needs to know about me.

This must be a good thing as, should I ever get lost, it would track me down in no time. Sadly, I accept that I am no longer a name with a personality that has all those odd human traits and appendages attached to it. Mind you, in my eyes, the same applies to the bank, which, when I call up, is now just a maze of computer-driven prompts or a jumble of corporate promotions on a computer screen, an amorphous mass without a human face.

As things stand, there is no longer a branch manager I can communicate with to disparage or even to convey my appreciation. Computer identification or not, I would have thought there should have been a human being somewhere in the branch, department, or whatever it is, who just may have heard of me. However, having recently adjusted my thinking, I don't think there is, and I reckon, just to make sure that I do not ask my branch manager out for dinner, his branch no longer appears in the phone book nor can I bring it up on my computer screen.

A Tennis Match

Each weekend, for years, I played tennis with the same group of friends. We were young, married couples bringing up our children. There was parkland and a playground area near the courts, so you can picture the scene, the children running around and playing on the nearby slippery dip and swings, while the parents kept an eye on them. This story is about one of those parents, a very nice young father and a friend of mine, whom we shall call Harvey. He had a stutter that became quite pronounced when he was overanxious, which implies that he may have been anxious all the time, or perhaps even neurotic, which, let me assure you, he was not; but at the same time, his life had not exactly been an easy one.

Harvey was a young widower with children, whom he battled on bravely to raise on his own. Sandy, his adored young wife, had fallen a victim to breast cancer. As for his stutter, by it, you could gauge how his week had been. We could be playing a hard match—and he did like to win—and he might wish to dispute a line call or make a comment, which would come out as, 'tat's ats ats ats ats,' which was as far as he got. That impediment would be more evident if he'd had a difficult week, but he was a pretty good player and knowing him as we did, we could guess at what he wanted to say.

When everything at home and at work was fine, and he was in a familiar setting, he could talk about anything; and if you were an outsider, you would never be aware of any speech impediment. Harvey had a demanding job as a civil engineer, so doing that and raising three young children was no small undertaking.

Therefore, our tennis and the familiar connection it brought were very important to him. Then, as the children got older, it became clear that he was looking around for a wife, a search his friends happily assisted in. This led to some mixed results, but nonetheless, the thought was there. This was a talking point, a quest that bound us together, and often kept us frustrated or highly amused, and you could say it was a search we felt privileged to be a part of.

Those early years must have been tough, and we saw it as a very promising sign when the quest began. His children were looking good, and the storm clouds were behind them. Some of that had to do with their friends, who had stepped in. Between them, the young mothers had a roster of who picked or dropped off the children; and in the evening, they were bathed and fed, which continued for as long as it was needed.

So it was, that in quick succession, we met an Emerald, a June, a Kay, and a Penny, as he trotted them out to see our reaction and might say, "she was very nice, didn't you think?" For my part, I always gave an encouraging response, knowing that when the right lady came along, nature would take its course. But I have to say one or two of the wives had given a young hopeful match named Nancy, a very prompt thumbs down, which was the only time I ever saw it happen. Apart from our own efforts, what kept us intrigued was to learn of the source of this steady flow of ladies, as we watched the ebb and flow of his budding romances.

If they turned up at tennis at all, and he invited them back again, that was a promising sign. Occasionally they could actually play, which was even better. That Christmas, Harvey produced a new lady named Carol; by Easter there was Anita, and on it went, until Margaret arrived. She stayed on the scene much longer than most, and began to emerge as a front runner. She was not a tennis player; however, she enjoyed the friendly atmosphere and we thought she was a pleasant and well-meaning young lady. Margaret had an opinion on most things—including houses, gardens, and the suburbs she liked—and made occasional forays into the rearing of children; so we were in no doubt where she had set her sights.

But Harvey was special to us, and the feeling arose that she was not the one; the women, especially, could not see her with him or his children. He never asked me and I accepted that it was probably only a fling, and I would not make a comment one way or the other. However, this affair had lasted much longer than normal.

Then an angelic apparition appeared in the form of a delightful young lady named Helen, who, besides all her other attributes, and there were many, played tennis like a dream, and was liked by everyone. As this promising relationship progressed, Harvey wore a look of happiness and lust that was unmistakable. This lasted through the spring, when, just as suddenly as she had been brought into our lives, she disappeared. There followed a Deirdre and a

Gayle in quick succession, with brief appearances of Margaret in between.

Then one day at tennis, Helen reappeared as if there had never been an absence. It may have been just before lunch when Margaret arrived, completely unaware of who Helen was. Setting out to introduce them, Harvey said, "tis dis dis dis dis dis," but he could get no further, and someone did it for him. During the next set, which paired Harvey and Helen, whether one of the ladies may have let on, or she had decided she may have intruded, Margaret had quietly slipped away.

That set was a hard one, with the games locked at five-all, and with the score at deuce, my partner served to Harvey. He returned it firmly to the forehand, and it went back to his forehand, which he returned and which I intercepted at the net, and my shot, which I placed between our opponents, may have been just over the baseline. Then in a clear and unhesitating voice, he sang out, "Sorry old son, but that shot was out by a country mile." In that moment, the same thought occurred to my partner and me, and we gave each other a high five, knowing our Harvey had finally met his match.

A Song for a Trooper

I woke up in Ward Seven and found myself encased in a plaster cast from my chest down. My bed was on the ground floor and at the front of St Vincent's Hospital in the inner Sydney suburb of Darlinghurst. Outside, I could see a row of grey columns, some of the park opposite, including an old, timber band rotunda, the bobbing hats of tall people as they walked by, and the buses and cars going up and down the road that went up the hill on the other side of the park. From where I lay, the ward ceiling seemed at least twenty feet high; the windows were nearly as tall, always open; and on summer days, you could feel the cooling breeze on your skin.

There were lines of beds against the wall on either side of the ward. The foot of each bed faced one on the other side. In the middle of the ward, there was a desk, which served as a nursing station. Waking up to find myself in an orthopedic ward came as a shock. The fellow in the bed on my right was young man of about my age, named Michael, who had a strange-looking steel traction device attached to his skull. But before you shrink in horror, as I did, it was possibly life-saving, and he said he could not feel it. This stretching apparatus was held taut by a cable which ran through a pulley at the head of the bed and had weights attached to the end of it. There he spent all day lying flat on his back, staring at the ceiling.

The bed on the other side held Richard, who, while I was there, would get a little more movement and feeling in his upper body and graduate to a wheel chair. He had a wife and three little children who came to visit.

My doctor was a tall, elegant man with a tanned and craggy face and a confident manner.

"I have put you in a radical plaster cast," he explained, "it will be uncomfortable at first, but you will get used to it. I want to keep you immobilized, so the bone will knit; so do try and keep still, and I want you to drink plenty of milk."

My broken femur (the big bone above the knee) seemed an insignificant problem when compared with my neighbor's. I don't recall ever hearing Michael complain, and in fact, he made a joke of how he had headed a ball during a game of what the rest of the world call football, and which Australians know as soccer, and found he could not move. Richard said a wheat auger had fallen on him. He would have been in his early forties, had dark hair and a pleasant face, with deep lines across his forehead.

When hospitalized, I reverted to what now seems to me have been a childlike institutionalized mental state. I remember it as being quite carefree. It has never been explained to me, and I assume we revert to it in order to cope with situations beyond our control. Looking back, I hope I was not a nuisance to the staff, particularly the nurses. Nurse Mary Sheridan got me through that first night, checking on me, soothing and reassuring, and getting the Sister to give me a shot of morphine. That was like riding a magnificent winged horse up into the clear blue sky and never having to come down again. I think I can understand addiction, and a fortnight or so later, although I did not know what they were, being pacified, as I was, with pain killers and calmatives, I am pretty sure I went through the classic withdrawal symptoms.

Nurse Sheridan was slightly higher than the height of the creamed steel headboard; she might have been described as nougatty, but she really wasn't. She had a friendly face with unblemished skin. Her hair disappeared upwards beneath a starched white hat and she had sandy eyebrows and pleasant eyes. As they all were, she was immaculately turned out; I would say "scrubbed" as they would have called it in those times.

The nurses wore polished black shoes, black stockings, a short-sleeved white-and-blue striped dress with white collar, matching cuffs, and a starched white pinafore, worn over it, which did its best to hide their femaleness. Around their waist, there was a wide blue-and-white belt with a shiny stainless steel buckle. I never saw them any other way.

Nurse Sheridan lifted us, sat us on our pans and wiped our bums, and fetched steel containers, known as "bottles", for us to urinate in. Mary always had something nice to say and looked after us as if we were babies.

"Geoffrey, you have not eaten your porridge; porridge is good for you; never mind, it is cold now; eat some toast and jam."

"Mary, my plaster stinks."

"Put some talc down it, and stop complaining. Michael does not complain, do you Michael?"

"No, but that is only because I am deeply in love with you Mary."

"Don't be stupid. Michael, I know there has been a steady procession of young ladies in to see you; so don't talk nonsense."

"But I am. I love you much more than any of them."

"No he doesn't Mary; he says that to all the nurses, and the fact is I love you more than Michael does."

"Now Geoffrey, you're being just as stupid."

"Boys, it is bath time now; be sure to wash yourselves thoroughly."

Nurse Sheridan returned with my basin and did the parts I could not reach, and after I had shaved, cleaned my teeth and combed my hair. I felt quite civilized. Then she rolled Michael over and carefully washed him as the flow of good-humored banter continued.

"Nurse, if these boys are bothering you," Richard might say, "just give me the word and I will individually straighten them out for you."

It was pure, if strange, hospital humor.

Occupational therapist Angela Sweeney wore a plain white uniform, although no uniform could be called plain with her in inside it; she had long blond bangs down to her shoulders, a glowing face, lovely brown skin, and a distinctive husky voice.

"Today," she said, "we are going to make a stool. I will give you each a frame, and we will start by weaving the seat, trying not to make too much of a mess as we do so. Now, watch carefully as I show you how it is done. If we are all finished when I come next Thursday, we will paint the frames. They can be yellow, dark blue, or black, so think about that. Hello Michael, how are you today? Would you like me to read you a story?"

"Hello Angie, I have missed you. How have you been?"

"Terrific, thanks. The choice for today is 'Death in the High Sierras' or 'Ric Calhoun's Last Ride'. Go for the first one; it has more corpses per page, and I find it easier to read."

"Angie, did I tell you that you remind me of Grace Kelly, although I prefer you any day?"

"Michael, I heard confidentially that you only have eyes for Nurse Sheridan; so I don't believe a word you say; so for goodness sake, be quiet and let me begin."

I spent more time listening to her than I did weaving my seat. After thirty minutes or so, she said, "Michael, I am sorry but I have to go to another ward." Then turning to me, "perhaps Geoffrey could finish the story for you," which I did. Having been given the cue, I got into the habit of reading everything aloud, particularly sporting magazines and the daily newspapers.

Someone had given me one of those small 'Boomerang' song books, which were very popular at the time. They had the words to all the popular songs. Thus Mario Lanza was given a big workout, and really slaughtered, as were Doris Day, Perry Como, Mitch Miller, and Frank Sinatra, and a great many other popular vocalists. Passing Doctors, nurses, and patients would put their heads in the door to see what all the din was about. Nonetheless, we persevered and most mornings, held a sing-a-long, so that in time, actually, we thought we sounded pretty good.

Judith Maloney was one of our physiotherapists. She had a big voice, a raucous laugh, and gave a running commentary as she worked.

"Geoffrey has not done his exercises because he is too lazy; and how do I know? Well, because it's my job, and I have to say I am very disappointed?"

"He is a well-known malingerer," came from somewhere down the other end.

"Judith, why don't you throw him out, so we can get some peace and quiet around here; and anyway, he is taking up a valuable bed," Richard had thrown in for good measure.

"He has one more chance to redeem himself; and now we will do twenty leg flexes together; one flex, hold it, release, two, again flex, that's it, release."

When she had finished with me and Richard, she would be joined by Margarita Delores, who had a nice smile, was tall, and in comparison with her, had a quiet personality. They would put a screen around Michael and start working. They pummeled, kneaded, stretched, bent, and folded; neatly turned him over, and did it all again on the other side.

One day, after telling everyone loudly what a hopeless case I was, Judith lent across so she was close to my ear and whispered that Michael had tingles in his legs, and what a good sign it was. I said a little prayer, and willed it to be, and when I got the opportunity, I told Richard.

Nurse Claire Knudsen came on duty in the afternoons. She was about a head higher than the bed head, had beautifully defined cheek bones, and a nice smile that was never far away. There were a few wayward strands of hair that spilt from under her hat. She had to blow these wisps out of her eyes whenever she bent over. She was statuesque, and moved like a dancer; she was pinched at the waist and it was more than her uniform could do to disguise her figure. She was a third-year nurse with three stripes and came from Casino—the coastal town in northern New South Wales, and I felt that if she came from there, it had to be a nice place. I can recall that when she had her back to me, she had the loveliest ankles and calves.

Claire was my dream, and Michael's and Richard's, and I spent a great deal of time thinking about what scintillating things I was going to say to her when she next came on duty. My excess fat and muscle under my skin were fast disappearing, and if I peered down into my cast, I could see daylight when I breathed in.

The daily sing-a-long began early in the morning, when Richard wheeled his chair around, so he was facing Michael and me, and with the song book in one hand, he conducted with the other. Mary, Judith, Delores, and the adorable Angela, of the occupational therapy, and the golden bangs, were serenaded with their very own love songs. But for the object of our affection, we had chosen a song called "Bewitched", which we were still perfecting, the words being modified so her name and a few other nice things we wanted to tell her came into it. Also, we were attempting a little counter harmony, and trying to sound like the Mills brothers.

"Knudy", as she was affectionately known, told us what was happening in the real world, and what was "in" and what was "out", what films she had seen, and where she had been. Then as a late night treat, she might fetch us hamburgers, or fish and chips, from somewhere up the road. The big day for the launch of her song was fast approaching, and we were working on our harmony, hand movements, grooming, and dress for the big occasion. But that Monday morning, when Mary arrived with her usual breezy greeting, and peals of laughter at our corny performance, the usual banter flowed back and forth freely, and as she was helping me get organized for the day and, as I usually did, I asked her, "And Mary, what was the highlight of your weekend?"; to which she replied with excruciating candor, "Claire Knudsen's engagement party; she and Doctor Jim Swain are getting married, and we all had a marvelous time."

But the show must go on no matter what; and I wore a bow tie and a borrowed jacket; Richard wore sports trousers, a Sinatra hat, and a wide tie with a palm tree painted on it. Michael was just being

Michael, but for this occasion, although he never wore shirts, he had one draped over him with a tie sitting in the right place. It was at the end of the second verse and during the chorus where we sang, "And nevertheless we are in love with you," that my tears came, which with the audience gathered around, made the inappropriateness and poignancy of our performance seem much worse than perhaps it was.

But the nurse of our collective, if doomed, desire was a trouper; she never missed a beat, did all the right things, applauded madly, pretended she had not noticed a thing, and told us how flattered she was, and how much our song had meant to her.

The Interview

I am one of those who have an aversion to those over-marketed motivational "How To" books. I particularly dislike those that purport to tell us how to prepare for and conduct ourselves during that all-important interview for a job. As I imagine, the authors make more money selling their books than they ever did while holding down a proper job of their own. These days, I don't take job interviews too seriously, as I am inclined to wonder whether there really is a job, and if there is, if someone already on the staff has been selected.

With all this proliferation of advice, it is little wonder that most job interviews turn out to be much the same. I find that if I don't put myself out, I get the job, and then have to decide if I really want it. Then again, if I put my heart and soul into it, I usually don't get to first base. However, I feel the process can put us through a great deal of stress.

Take my own case. Having left a quiet life in the country, I had arrived in Sydney, an earnest young man, ready to make my mark in the world. And I can remember being very put off during my first interview. The chap on the other side of the desk was, in complete contrast to myself, self-assured, polished, and spoke as though he knew absolutely everything. I imagined that he would have been rapidly climbing up through the ranks of his company. And fair enough. And I will admit to feeling awkward, gangly, and unsophisticated.

There followed the worst of all possible outcomes, as my interviewer had a hyphenated name, a phenomenon which I had never seen before. Now, I have no idea if they were a rarity in those days, but as you know, today practically every second person you meet has one, and the world seems full of Smith-Merringtons,

Woodly-Browns, and Cecil-Appletons. I cannot imagine what will happen should they choose to intermarry?

My interviewer's name was something like Carrington Todd-Farcombe, which I never quite caught when we were introduced. Being unsure and nervous are dreadful conditions; this was all about me wanting to be a wool buyer, considered a very glamorous occupation in those days. But this interview would never get off the ground. The questions had started, and I had already forgotten the order of his name. Was it Farcombe Carrington-Todd? Was his first name Todd? Confusion reigned; no, it was Farcombe, and I dared not use any of them.

Such confusion over a name, but in this, I was not alone. A young lady friend of mine was a representative for a pharmaceutical company. And despite her best efforts, she could never get a deal going with a potential customer, a Mr. Magintry—an unusual name I grant you. This Magintry character was apparently a very sharp operator, and my friend's company was desperate to get his business; she was under all sorts of pressure, but could never swing it.

I can't give you the details, as we lost contact, and it was some years later before our paths crossed again, and by then, my friend had risen through the company hierarchy. This would have been at one of those industry seminars so beloved by multinational corporations. We were enjoying a drink and I asked how she ever got on with her would-be customer. "Oh, I remember, you mean Frank Macintyre; he's going great guns, thank you. Someone in the head office got his name muddled which was just one of those screw-ups that happen in big companies"

Perhaps we should consider the time, when, as a young man full of self-worth and idealism, I saw where the Australian Government was recruiting young people with a rural background for our trade missions abroad. I knew right away what I wanted to be. I wrote them a beautiful letter, which, if anything, modestly expounded my experience and qualifications, and then sat back to wait for their reply.

As you would expect, theirs was a very official reply, which came on a fully embossed letter contained in a thick snow-white envelope.

"Would I kindly present myself to be interviewed by members of the selection board etc?" it went on to say.

Was there, could there be, anyone else? I actually read articles about prawn fishing up in the Gulf, cane harvesting, tomato varieties and their cultivation, and the techniques of mohair production on marginal land, just for my own amusement.

On the morning of my interview, a number of other earnest young men were also waiting. "Giles T.R.", announced one of those serious-faced ladies who abound in such place). A pasty-faced chap, whose collar was far too big, got up and disappeared down the corridor, trailing behind her. "Longbottom J.T." followed, until it eventually came to me.

The Sydney interviews were held in a boardroom on the top floor of an office building in Pitt St, near the intersection of Hunter Street, and everything about the venue was impressive. The lifts were big enough to hold a small truck. There was absolute silence, and nothing moved along the wide corridors. The selection panel was seated on the other side of the long boardroom table, and there was a fabulous view of the city and the harbor behind them. I steeled myself—*how could it be anyone else?*

Among the people was a hatchet-faced man, sitting opposite, who had a cowlick and big ears, just like Sam, our milkman. Sam was a friend of my father's who always came into our place for a few beers early on Christmas morning. But, as it turned out, this chap's personality was not like Sam's at all, and I think I may have misread their welcoming smiles?

What those serious faces were trying to tell me would have been something like this, "we are a selection board made up of the most senior public servants you are ever likely to meet. Further, we are going to select only the very finest, as we search for those worthy of a second interview. When we have made our choice, they will go forward and work with all the authority of the Australian Government. Indeed, they will have the whole nation behind them as they win enormous orders for our produce in Cairo, Singapore, Shanghai, and Lima."

I do recall that you tend to fantasize at that age.

Meanwhile, hopefully, they would have noticed that my hair was slicked down and cut in the mandatory short back-and-sides style, which was the only cut the nation's barbers were familiar with. Fortunately, they would not notice that my white shirt was so over-starched that it was chafing me in the most uncomfortable places, and they would have seen that there was not a pimple in sight. They would have seen that my tie was not so loud that it drew attention to itself; yet, was not so insipid that people might think me indecisive. They would also see that the trouser creases of my gunmetal suit were two knife edges, and the slits in the back of my jacket were somewhat reminiscent of a younger Duke of Edinburgh. To achieve the desired effect, I had tried on every tie in the house, and had polished my shoes until I could see my face in them. I was ready to take on the world.

I will pause here to point out that a young man on the way up can be greatly influenced by the career paths of his mates. One of mine was a young Dane, who was living the high life in Sydney while doing a similar job for his country. I had seen it with my own eyes. Young ladies literally threw themselves at his feet; so you can see the connection.

It is also my experience that you learn early in life that some apparatuses should never have been invented, like the Mark One Calf Marking Machine, which I invented. The idea still seems very feasible. This was a simple, lever action affair that only needed the addition of a safety catch. I will not elaborate further, in case anyone reading this has the same nasty accident. This slight design fault did not prevent the handle releasing and knocking out a front incisor tooth. Mind you, the way the dentist had fashioned its replacement, I don't think you would ever know.

That accident came back to haunt me, as I recall another job interview with a very nice chap, who was also the Managing Director. The interview was held in a smart office building in Young St. At the time, I was living above a ferry wharf in Mosman Bay, and I would catch the ferry back into the city. About halfway through the interview, I had been offered a cup of tea and a biscuit, when, to my horror, I discovered that I had forgotten to put my tooth in.

But we digress. As I sat opposite Sam, the milkman's look-alike, I must have checked every few seconds that I was wearing my false tooth. Their questions began with a few simple ones, which I handled with ease. Then the subject turned to apples and pears, with fairly routine questions on those.

It has been my experience that if you listen carefully, you can almost anticipate the odd trick question before it is asked. Suddenly, they switched to the export of citrus, that is, oranges and lemons, and I thought it was a red flag that it must be this. Sometimes, just like Winston Churchill, you are the man for the moment, which was how I felt.

I had a friend who was in warehousing, and he had given me a crash course about pallets, collapsible crates, and all that sort of thing. Also, I had only recently got up very early to visit the Sydney wholesale fruit and vegetable market to see it in operation. Then, mid interview, they suddenly altered course, "Assume you have an order for fifty tons of best quality Granny Smith apples to be delivered ASAP to Hong Kong. Please explain to the board how this order should be executed so they arrive quickly and unblemished?"

At that point, I had a vivid picture of myself with a fabulous redhead on one arm, and a stunning brunette on the other. I was smoking a Havana cigar and was checking the arrival of crates in Rotterdam, or was it Buenos Aires, prior to jetting off to an urgent meeting to discuss a much bigger deal over a scotch or two in Glasgow?

My definitive answer was given with absolute confidence, wrapping it up with a few pertinent observations of my own. What was this, the collective eyebrows across the table were raised, their heads were down and they were making furious notes?

What on earth had I done?

Their letter was polite; they thanked me for my application, and in a nice touch, wished me every good wish for the future. Some weeks later, I read in the press that the ban on the export of Australian apples to Hong Kong had just been lifted.

Part III -
Middle Years

Manhattan Lady

It came as a shock to me to discover that, as little boys go, I was very tidy and embarrassingly well-trained in housework; I mean in doing tasks like drying and washing the dishes, boiling up the laundry, rinsing it, and hanging it out to dry on the clothes line. As a matter of fact, I thought all little boys did things like that. My mother ran her home with much delegation and a firm hand. She had three children to bring up while our father was fighting for freedom, Winston Churchill, and King George V1, while she ran a corner grocery shop in Double Bay, a suburb of Sydney.

The habits of childhood are still with me today, when I find myself compulsively looking in the laundry basket to see if I should put a load on, things like that. When I visited my young school friends and found they just threw their dirty socks and other items of used clothing on the floor, and their mothers dutifully picked them up without a word, I could barely believe it. What sheer amazement when, in the morning, their mothers also served us breakfast in bed.

A very muddled view of life I suppose; a large dose of "cleanliness is next to Godliness", if you like; but I guarantee that once it is there, imbedded in a little boy's brain, he will never get rid of it. Many years later, in what seemed like a biblical revelation, all this knowledge of the ins and outs of good housekeeping came to me in a rush. I was well into the far end of middle age, inclined to take a benevolent view of the world, and particularly of young married couples, just setting out in their struggle for success, in much the same way as my wife and I had done.

However, something very profound had happened to the female half of the population. I cannot pinpoint exactly when this took place, but it may have been sometime in the late 1970s and was a fact of life by the 1990s. My mother had always been liberated, so you could say that much of the women's movement was lost on me.

Yet, it was much written about and commented upon, and when it was over, the change in women's attitudes came upon me with a shock.

There were no outward signs of the women's movement at our place, unless unbeknownst to me my wife was meeting in a secret cell. Let me put the whole thing into perspective by saying that having had wonderful women in my life, including our lovely daughters, I am all for equal opportunities for women in every field, and as far as I can recall, I always have been.

Looking back, I can see the invention of the contraceptive pill must have been the catalyst; but that was so long ago that I had almost forgotten. But there was more to it, and suddenly, government policies aiming at the advancement of women were introduced. There were books and protest marches, and stirring women's songs were sung and feature films were made. Women had linked arms in a worldwide movement; and a glorious thing it was!

The other thing, before we get too deeply into the subject, I confess to having a liking for females in uniform. Don't ask me where that stems from, but nonetheless, it is there. You understand, therefore, that for me, a nicely proportioned lady, striding confidently forward, attired in what is now universally known as a "power suit", has the completely opposite effect than what its wearer may have intended. Intimidated or impressed I am not; invariably attracted I am.

This observation may be straying from the point. However, it is fair to say that, like everyone else, I have become conditioned to all this change, so that when I saw a woman thus attired, I knew precisely what she was signaling to the world. I had better first explain that I used to have a suburban real estate business, an important part of which was leasing and managing houses. And on behalf of our owner clients, we used to like leasing them to smart young couples, "on the way up", so to speak.

They might be transferred to Sydney from Singapore, London, or New York—polished young husbands and their equally polished wives, who, together, generated huge incomes as international bankers with great multinational corporations, and so forth.

One day, when I was sitting in my office, busy with the morning paper and sipping a cup of tea, I received a very serious complaint. This charmingly-mannered and delightful-looking young lady and her husband had recently arrived from Manhattan. Such tenants, in my eyes, were absolutely terrific; he was a pale-faced young man with a serious air while she was important in the international market for stocks and bonds, and really knew what made the world go round.

Her arrival at my office that morning had been heralded by a brief but strident demand for service, as only Americans, particularly New Yorkers, know how to do. All this at the startled lady manning the front office, and before I could get up to see what the trouble may have been, our visitor had marched straight into my office and was standing on the other side of my desk, talking very loudly and pointing an accusing finger right in my face.

That morning she was beautifully attired in a well-cut suit, which was a slightly darker shade than straw; there was a touch of green running through it, that is, if we could ignore her strident manner for a moment. She also had short, bobbed auburn hair, a pale-yellow blouse under her coat, and two strands of, what I thought were, pearls, sitting up high around her lovely neck. I can recall that the effect she had on me was immediate, and again, if we ignore her manner, one of sheer delight; and I got up to show my great concern for her wellbeing.

Even her tirade could not detract me from my admiration; and the way they were presented, her complaints sounded serious. After her opening salvo had subsided, and she was by then sitting by the opposite corner of my desk, in a position, which, when I was seated behind it myself, seemed one to produce intimidation. However, I ignored all that and made a studious list of her complaints, nodding my head in agreement, or shaking it in sympathetic disgust.

You never knew with these situations. When they had moved in, everything in the house had been working like a dream, and the interior and the garden had been immaculate. I had been genuinely appalled at her list, and immediately returned with her to the house to ensure these frightful disasters were rectified straight away.

There was no question about it; Americans demanded service, and as they were usually paying for it, I made sure they got it. True, more than once I changed the entire color scheme of a house for the wife of a Regional President. I recall listening to the outpourings of one poor lady who was sick of her family being dragged all around the world, and very homesick for her own home, which had sounded very nice, and evidently outside of Chicago.

However, to return, things in her home did not look good; in the main living rooms, there were odd bits of clothing and other personal items lying around as if that morning, several visitors had left in a hurry. My experienced eye picked up those things my own mother would not have approved of: the layer of dust on the dining table, on the sideboards and on the window sills.

The carpet needed a good vacuuming, there being patches of talcum powder in the passageways, and other unfavorable signs, none of which she made any comment about, nor were they on her list. On the top of hers had been the bad condition of the bathrooms, the pooling of water, and numerous other complaints. And I could do nothing but agree, as in their state then, the bathrooms were a disgrace. We continued to the kitchen which I could hardly recognize as the one I knew.

Julia was calming down… we will call her Julia… as it happens to somehow match my fond memory of her, and believe me, I was treading very carefully as this young lady knew how to command respect. Yet, nowhere had I seen a broom, a duster, a mop, or any other of those well-known items, including packs of proprietary cleaners, which my wife had, or dare I admit, a well-trained little boy had been taught by his mother long ago, to use for house cleaning.

I was starting to worry, when we fortunately came upon a montage of impressively framed photographs hanging on a wall in the living room; they were of her wedding. She and her husband made a very handsome couple.

"Lovely dress," I commented. It was, and I have to say so was the young bride wearing it, "and Julia," I asked, "when was that taken?"

"Thank you, oh, I guess just a couple of months before we came over," she replied wistfully.

"Now Julia," I said, "I sincerely regret what has happened to your home, and I am going to see that it is made just the way you want it. This afternoon I am going to send around a couple of professional house cleaners who will get it all sparkling and new again. After that, I suggest they come once a week, so they can keep your home just the way you want it. We will run this on your account. The first clean will be more expensive than a normal weekly visit, but once a week after that should be fine."

"Oh no, I couldn't possibly do that," she said, quite alarmed at my suggestion, and in that moment, power suit, the sophisticated and often hitherto imperious manner, and the very certainty of her existence in the world, came tumbling down. "I promised my husband that I could handle the house on my own, but right now, he is very annoyed with me." She was very upset and flushed. "It is just not fair," she sobbed, "and I am learning to cook, but a nice home should never get like this, should it?"

Had she been able to witness it, my mother would have been extremely satisfied. That morning, Julia and I went shopping for squeeze mops, dusters, buckets, brooms, and all the rest of it, including a vacuum cleaner. Later, in a coffee shop, we made a list of all the housekeeping jobs, including, in the true spirit of the women's movement, some for her young husband to do. I for one would never have wished to change her; a modern liberated woman or not, as I found out, there had always been a protective mother and maids in her life, so what more could her new young husband expect?

It comes back to me now that when we returned to her home, while having a pleasant conversation about her life and with me assuming the role of an expert, we started on the kitchen. Then, having dealt with the basics, moved on to the worst bathroom, where in the manner of a professional, I could stand back and throw in some practical coaching. Of course I never told her, but her list was just like the one my mother had drawn up and hung so prominently at a little boy's height on the side of the dresser in our kitchen.

Donkeys at the Races

Getting all dressed up and going to the races is a very civilized thing to do. Ladies especially like the opportunity to dress up, and might show off a new hat, and of course they like to see what the other ladies wear for the occasion. What could be more pleasant, particularly if you happened to know of a good horse and the weather is kind? There are the flower beds to admire, and the opportunity to have a good look at the horses, chatting to old friends, and perhaps sharing a glass of champagne when someone's horse comes home.

At country race meetings, everyone knows everyone else, and they all know of an "absolute certainty", which, in my experience, has rarely ever won. Once I followed a very well-known owner around a country race meeting. He was a very pleasant and well-thought-of chap, who spoke to everyone and knew all about horses. He would be followed by an admiring retinue that drank in his every utterance. I remember that he certainly punted like mad, and I never saw him win a thing, which was a very useful lesson to an impressionable young man like me.

When I was working out in the Australian bush, it was pleasant to get out of my dusty work clothes and dress up and go to the races. Like the other young men, I also went to meet up with our lady friends. Never mind the heat and the flies, this was just another opportunity for some pleasant social interaction, which, on a property miles out of town, could be in short supply.

You might not have been aware, but it is perfectly true that horsy people do talk to their horses. Not about politics, or if it might rain, or whether that year's wheat crop will be any good. Mostly it will be routine comments like, "stand still; good boy, back up now; steady while I lift your leg," or other encouraging things spoken softly while rubbing and patting. It takes place while saddling, grooming, shoeing, opening a gate, or coming up to a jump. I have often done it myself.

The phenomena like the equine psychology of the "Horse Whisperer", as depicted in the film, and the discovery that the way a horse's head is held may limit its vision, particularly over a jump, only add to the potential of the relationship. I like horses very much, but I am certainly no expert. Let me tell you what I know about horses: they should not be allowed to get too fat; never feed them too much of a single grain in a narrowly-based diet, which particularly applies to wheat; and like humans, they need a balanced ration, clean water, companionship, adequate shelter, and of course, plenty of exercise.

Unfortunately, it is still not possible to hold a normal conversation with a horse, which, in my view, is a shame. Wouldn't it be nice to be able to sidle up to a horse at a race meeting, and when no one was looking, have a man-horse dialogue that might go something like this:

"Good morning Stella Lass, I trust you are feeling well-rested today?"

"Thank you for asking, but no. I was having a lovely dream at four o'clock this morning, when that fool of a groom came in and woke me up before I was put through a strenuous gallop over 1000M, so if you want to know, I am tired, stiff, and in a really lousy frame of mind."

"You are in the fifth today over 1500M. How do you think you will go?"

"I am not the slightest bit interested. I don't like the jockey, an ill-tempered little man if ever there was one, and, as I said, I am just not in the mood. But seeing you asked, have a talk with Daisy three boxes along, that's 'Nirvana Belle', but for goodness sake, don't call her that; she can't stand her registered name. The other girls have decided she should win; she has been so down lately since being given the brush-off by 'Wilandra Boy', otherwise known as Fred, who is only a gelding, you know; but still, you cannot blame a girl for dreaming."

"Thanks. Have a couple of sugar cubes and a carrot."

"You're welcome."

Our potential communication with horses is worth working on, but in the meantime, I really don't take them too seriously. I will admire their conformation and the way they move, but apart from that, I am not in the business of trying to read their minds. Besides, I am all for privacy; but mind you, I have had a few wins at the races.

One such occasion comes to mind.

My idea of an enjoyable day at the races is a nice sunny day, and to get there early. I also like good company, and the opportunity to get close to the horses. And I am really thrilled, when one I particularly like gets up and wins. Maybe, and only maybe, if I am in the mood, and most of my criteria for a race have been met, I will have a small punt. You could say I am there for the fellowship, to see the horses, and to enjoy the spectacle.

However, on this particular day, my companion was a very successful property man, who was well known as a serious punter. There was also a mutual friend of ours who was a luminary of the motor industry, and who, I suspect, might have been trying to emulate our friend.

The property man was a pleasant, gregarious fellow, who had something to say about most things. Usually I like to look at the horses, admire the gardens, chat with my companions, and when the sun is high, enjoy a friendly pre-lunch drink. However, with these two, this was not to be; for one moment, we were chatting away, and the next, they had entered a huddle with a group of men of the race-track-tout variety, whom I studiously avoid. Having overheard their hushed discussion, which was of betting values and the reported opinions of their racing connections, I quickly lost interest.

Thereafter, and between races, my companions went straight to the betting ring, and this irritating behavior continued. As you can imagine, I did not enjoy the company, or the lack of it. However, out of interest, from time to time, I placed a small bet on the horse I fancied. Please understand that simply by pure chance, I was successful, so that by the end of the day, I had two wins and three of my other selections had come home for a place.

Later, the others joined me in the bar, and there was much talk of how, in their opinion, this or that horse or its jockey had not performed as they should have. And on and on they went, and I promised myself never to attend the races with them again.

"And how did you get on?" they asked me.

I told them.

"Typical beginners luck," they said.

"And you fellows?"

"Not bad, but it has not really been my day," said one.

"Quite well, but you know how it is with racing," said the other.

"I was wondering," said the property man, "if you would oblige me with a hundred dollars, just to tide me over for the day?"

"Yes, and I wonder could you do the same for me," asked the motor industry luminary.

Never a Memorable War

While researching material for a novel, in which one of the main characters is called up into the Army and serves in an infantry platoon in Vietnam, I was reminded that only a few years earlier, I had received a very pressing invitation to attend a reunion of former pupils of Sydney Grammar School, of which I was one.

This was a grand occasion in the function room of one of the city's leading hotels, and there was much chest thumping, with many famous and prominent old boys in attendance. But I had reservations, as I could not see how I could strike up a conversation about a school I had never really cared for in the first place, and not with men I had not seen for well over forty years.

I could not pretend otherwise, as I was never a happy and contented secondary school boy. When I was a little chap, I tended to be the king of the kids; but I felt out of my depth in the starchy atmosphere of a large grammar school. At the time, I would have been incapable of explaining why.

If I liked the masters, and they could teach, I did very well; otherwise my school work was poor. I enjoyed my school friends, playing cricket and football, military cadet camps, and things like that. However, as I look back, I find I must have learned more than I gave them credit for. I certainly came away with a useful smattering of French and Latin, and a little bit of everything else, as well as an abiding affection for modern and ancient history.

As for that reunion, I don't know how they did it, what with nearly a thousand of us in the one room to be fed and watered, which they did very well. We were spoken to by the august few, who had excelled in the law or other avenues of endeavor. Everyone would have been aware of those who had enjoyed great commercial success.

However, for the most part, I imagine those former pupils would have been just like myself. They had climbed no towering mountain, and were living an ordinary life out in the suburbs. I mention the law, because it seemed to me there were more members of that profession than any other calling; perhaps they gravitate to such functions.

For me, that evening was a step backwards in time. I suppose I still carried the baggage of a boy's distant schoolyard remembrances, the dislikes and prejudices, which had lingered in my mind. Some of the faces looked exactly the same, while others, I could barely recall. I had a delightful conversation with a fellow I remembered as being a complete brat, which did a lot to shake my certainty. Yet, at my table, the faces were fixed in that sorrowful time of life when men look back and realize they have achieved very little; and they wondered about their wasted years, while the conversation struggled to go anywhere.

There was no sign of my small circle of close school friends, whom, as much out of curiosity, I would have enjoyed meeting again. I wondered who had survived, and whether I would recognize them, or they me. I had surmised that if they had lived a life with the same zest and attitudes we had, when we were boys at school, they most likely would have succumbed to alcoholism, and all the other excesses a man might indulge in.

One could have been forgiven for thinking the evening had been arranged to promote the legal profession, as a prominent jurist droned on and on. They are always so highly thought of, and he regaled us with his view of the world. While I recalled that some of the most difficult and repugnant business dealings I ever had were with members of that profession. They are so certain of their views, as if there could be no other. I then shared a drink and a joke with a few friends I had met through the property industry, and I had decided to surreptitiously make an exit, when, just as I was about to leave, I saw an elderly teacher whom I admired, and decided I should make myself known.

He had been one of those nurturing figures in a boy's life who may not have been appreciated at the time. And yet, no doubt, like me, many former students would later come to realize what a great influence he had been. I would have introduced myself as a being from the year of nineteen fifty-four, whereas I was greeted with an astonishingly warm smile and handshake, as if my school days had ended the previous week.

How strange it felt to be addressing a former schoolmaster as an equal. Probably unnecessarily, I reminded him that he had taken me for modern history, and that I had been a member of the School Cadet Corps. He had obviously done this before, as there was a twinkle in the eye and a knowing look, as if the progress of one small school boy of years ago was vividly recalled.

"Nice of you to make yourself known," he said.

"I thought I ought to take the opportunity to tell you," I continued, "that it was not until I was called up for National Service in the Army that I discovered how well you had trained us, and I wanted to say thank you."

Although much older, he seemed not to have changed all that much, and making an educated guess, I came up with mid to late eighties. He had been a Major in the Second World War and had served in the Siege of Tobruk, the Battle of El Alamein, and later in New Guinea. After the war, he had returned to teaching and had lived, what I would call, a most useful life. We made the usual small talk, but how does a schoolmaster, whose very career must have spanned a vast sea of adolescent faces, even pretend to recall one average school boy from years ago? Of course he could not, unless they had been outstanding pupils, who had later become army generals, renowned surgeons, captains of industry or, perhaps, even High Court judges.

I had wanted to make a simple gesture of respect. In my mind were memories of parades, cadet camps, and scaled-down exercises orchestrated for school boys. It seemed to me that he had been dedicated to passing on the craft of soldiering, all the things that I had never appreciated at the time, but the value of which came to me so clearly some years later.

His military bearing was just as I remembered, and I could still picture him standing in front of a company of cadets, as he relived a battle for us with the aid of a sand pit and an unerring memory of the struggle's ebb and flow.

This ability to bridge the gap between adult and child must be a unique gift, for this teacher had made young boys feel like men, and many had gone on to distinguish themselves as professional soldiers. He conducted our Cadet Corps maneuvers as seriously as a theatre director, setting the atmosphere with the complete cooperation of the cast, building the tension, which climaxed in a full-scale and realistic exercise mounted at night. How else do you get boys in full military kit, ready in their precise positions for an infantry attack? I vividly recall a maneuver launched from a start line in the middle of the night, and in silence, using only the available moon and star light. Those school boys were eager to carry home their attack.

Memories like this made a vivid backdrop as we talked. I wondered how many other former pupils had taken the opportunity to express much the same thing. This elderly teacher and my father had fought in the same war, and it seemed to me that they had a very accepting, even a benevolent, good-humored attitude toward it. For my father, once it was over, it was best forgotten; whereas, I imagine, my former teacher may have viewed it through the eye of an historian. My conversation with him was the highlight of that school reunion.

I did not mention that I saw my time as a National Serviceman in the army as a fiasco, and that at no time did our unit ever approach the high standard of his Cadet Corps. So badly were we managed that the army seemed incapable of discovering that large quantities of our rations were being stolen right under its nose.

But, to return to my researching the operation of the Australian Army in the Vietnam War for my novel—the most poignant conversation about that war I ever had was with a former Warrant Officer who had served two tours. He had been severely wounded on the second. Somehow, I do not think my father or my former schoolmaster would have approved, as perhaps they were the last of the stiff-upper-lip followers of the Churchillian ideal. I had wanted to understand the Vietnam War because my fictional character gets severely wounded, which is the profound turning point in his life. So I had come to this interview in the hope of getting some authentic background.

However, the former Warrant Officer and I got off to a rocky start, as he turned up for our interview morosely drunk. This former soldier was the real deal, having been engaged in some very heavy fighting. Having survived his severe wounds, he was also a product of the army medical system, which had put him back together as best as it could. Our next interview never got off the ground, as again he had been drinking.

Now wiser, I hit upon the ploy of meeting him early in the morning, before too much self-harm could be inflicted, and the next interview did the trick. He answered with clarity, and we had a fruitful couple of hours talking about his service. I was grateful to have him as an eye witness, and I listened intently. His injuries had been horrific, and brought the admission that no Australian warrant officer would ever show fear in front of their men. In his view, and to their own detriment, they had begun to believe in their own immortality.

I was left with the impression that the fighting in Vietnam had been more intense, sudden, and violent than I had realized. I felt privileged to hear his account. I asked how he was coping. There was no self pity, "Things are not too bad; that war cost me my health and my marriage. But there is no point in complaining. I get a decent pension, but it is a pity that I can't concentrate enough to play bowls anymore. And as you already know, I like a drink; so I am not complaining."

About a month or so later, he and I met while shopping in the supermarket.

"Oh," he said with a smile, "and I did not tell you that these people also give me a handy discount."

Looking for my Brother

This is an excerpt from my novel *The Dust of their Dreaming*, which follows the lives of two indigenous Australian children who spent their early childhood on a remote cattle station. We join them after Darain has lost his wife to cancer.

~~~

"I know I am not the first to have to do this, but my brother had learned to live in the street. I watched him share a bottle with a man with grey whiskers; empty bottles of port and dry sherry lay in the gutter around them. He had no idea I was there. After searching frantically for two nights, finally I had found him. The sight of him in that appalling state upset me; he was lying in a dingy lane like a dirty pile of old rags. Quietly, I crept away to race for my car before he could move on again. He was light and he stank, and I bundled him into the back of the car. I had chosen the coast road in the hope it would gain me a few days to straighten him out. He needed to understand what was happening. There had been no recognition, and it surprised me that he could have reduced himself to this.

I found a motel on the coast with parking bays in front of the rooms, a few snips with my dressmaking shears and the stinking clothes came away. I wished he was with our father out in the bush. I placed a plastic chair under the shower and turned it on. His eyes were shut against the light; the face was thin; his chest caved as if he may have been starving to death. He had been hastened into old age. I soaped his head, and discovered the revolting sores and scabs. The water had turned grey. Now there was some resemblance. I trimmed fingernails and brushed his hair. He was very thirsty, and his breath and teeth were disgusting; and he coughed up most of his omelet.

He was too weak to protest. On the third day, we managed a walk down to the beach, and when he was tired, I put him to bed. The following day was much better; he understood what was

happening. The air was full of the sea as we walked along the shore,
letting the waves wash over our feet. The trunks of the coastal brush
had been bent and gnarled by the wind. I sang to Nan, telling her he
was going to recover. Things were going well until he suddenly
pleaded for a drink. I found that just too much.

"How dare you! You do this for Peggy; do it in memory of her.
Pull yourself together. I don't want to hear another word about
drink, heroin, or anymore of your pathetic self-indulgent nonsense."

I would drive for half a day, find a motel on the beach, endeavor
to get him to eat, then we would walk along the shore, and he would
sleep.

Slowly, we made our way north until it was our last day on the
coast, before I had to swing west along the banks of the Bellinger
River and up the cutting into the hills of New England. The deserted
beach stretched as far as I could see; the sand made a golden river
against the sea. The retreating waves filled our tracks.

"Dar, I am taking you to a place where there is no drink, and no
drugs, and you are going to find yourself. When you are recovered, I
will come and get you. Until then, you are to do as you are told.
Look at me. Peggy married a fine man, not a pathetic bum, who
would be a bloody nuisance to all those who love him."

As I spoke, the retreating water made little rivulets in the sand.

"Remember her with a clear head, and tell me you will do as they
say."

"Yes, I will."

"Your head has been full of Marmoo. I want us to enjoy our last
day at this pretty beach, because tomorrow I will take you there."

Dar could have been in a trance; normally, we would have
chatted about what we saw along the way, to me he appeared
bewildered. We drove through that lush country without comment
and on through the lovely rolling hills further on from Dorrigo.

"You will enjoy living in the country; it relaxes me, just seeing it
again. I wonder what Nan would have made of all this? Look, the
apple gums are in bloom, isn't it lovely?"

My brother said nothing.

"Nan would have missed us so much; she once told me that you
reminded her of Fritz. Please do not forget to sing to her and tell her
what you are doing; you will be able to see the stars much better up
here. Heather reckons the head of this place is charming; she went to
a great deal of trouble on our behalf. Look, the highway is gradually
falling away through the hills. This is more interesting than the flat

country; you will like this place. I believe it is in the foothills, so you might have a little of each."

At a junction, a sign directed me to the Dungowan Valley. There were pretty paddocks of lucerne flowers along each side of the gravel road. The hills were a hazy blue. An old red tractor cut a fresh brown swathe. The valley filled me with pleasure. Here and there, mobs of fat white sheep ate their way across the paddocks as I swung through the gate and parked under a tree in front of the Dunraven Priory.

"What a pretty setting!"

A row of magnificent pepper trees shed a carpet of pink seed around a lovely old sandstone building that reminded me of parts of Hunters Hill. The Abbot must have heard us as his beaming presence emerged and offered us a cheery greeting. He was the character monk straight out of a novel, complete with habit, a balding dome, and a bulging middle.

"Welcome to our Priory," he boomed, "I am Father David, and this fine gentleman must be your younger brother."

The moment was extraordinary; the rough brown habit appeared such an impractical garment for such a warm a day. There were splotches of animal dung and earth down the front; and as I later discovered, it was made of coarse woven wool. Grubby toes protruded from stout-looking sandals. A wide leather belt held the girth in place. He was nut brown and I thought that what hair remained may have once been sandy. This bear of a man was going to embrace me, and when he did, the smell was of assorted animals, and sweat. His hands were like hard leather; there would be no trouble keeping my brother in line. The Abbot was quite overwhelming.

"Darain, you and I are going to become the best of friends."

With this, he had grasped my brother's hands with both of his, as if this first meeting was special for them. But it was wasted on Dar. The Abbot's voice had a timber that could have been an opera singer's; and when it was lowered, the resonance was as smooth as syrup. His delivery brought back memories of evangelists, who had been so certain of everything; the Abbot would be a very persuasive man.

"Just a moment my dear lady, while I get your brother organized."

He had led us through the arched front door and across a flagged vaulted hall. His study was Spartan, and my heels' clip-clopping seemed inappropriate in such a place. There were two worn leather armchairs in one corner, but nothing that said anything about a former life—no family shot with elderly parents, no children, only posed black-and-white photos of monks adorned the walls.

"Say goodbye to your sister," and with that, Father David propelled my brother through the door, spoke to someone, and returned.

"Take my word, he will do well here; our loving God has been very good to deliver your brother."

I was not going to argue. His movements were surprisingly nimble as he slipped behind his desk.

"Believe me, you got him here just in time."

"Father David, I am sorry he is in such a dreadful state."

I was having serious doubts; any fire and brimstone preaching might break him. I had not felt this apprehensive since I was put in a different home. Father David smiled benevolently.

"Alkina, he and I are brothers in drink, may I assure you; we do understand. You are a wonderful caring sister, so he is much blessed. I was like him years ago; have no doubt he will be a different man. Shortly we will have a cup of tea; I am sure you could do with one. The thing is, my dear lady, they never seem to realize how much they intrude upon the lives of their family and friends. They live in complete self-absorption."

"I have noticed that when his wife was alive, I would never have believed this could possibly happen. Do you know the story?"

One of the cherubic-faced monks appeared, smiled pleasantly at her, and disappeared.

"I had a long chat with Heather, and what a wonderful friend she is, and she told me you are very special yourself. I mean we need to know what we are dealing with. His recovery will take time, but it is very satisfying when it happens."

The monk returned with a tea tray.

"Thank you Simon. Do try some of our bread and butter."

Brother Simon continued standing to one side.

"Our dear Simon used to be a successful pastry cook until he took to the demon drink and lost his way."

Simon smiled like a scolded child.

"Single-handed, our Simon declared war on the dear young men and women of the New South Wales Police Force. Fortunately for everyone, he lost. He bakes every day and we have the best bread this side of the Victorian border. I beg your pardon Simon, this dear lady is the elder sister of the man who has just this moment joined us. Peter is looking after him."

That comment must have been for their own information, as they smiled like a pair of conspirators. The bread was awful but I nibbled at it to be polite.

"No doubt, and right about now, they will be having a nice chat."

The Abbot's comment caused them to laugh.

"Perhaps Simon, you could get our guest some samples of our produce so she may rediscover just how good fresh food can taste."

The clear-eyed Simon wished me a safe trip and disappeared. The Abbot may have sensed my puzzlement.

"My dear, dear lady, that was very rude of me; we sometimes forget our visitors do not understand our humor. It was just that we knew your brother was rapidly being made aware that there are things to worry about other than himself. Almost without exception, that long-forgotten fact comes to many as a rude shock. Incidentally, thank you very much for your generous check."

Heather had very smartly discovered what might be required to get things moving.

"Your brother is to have no visitors for a while. When he is ready, he will contact you himself. At that time, I hope he will be something like the brother you remember. Have you time for a quick tour? Then we can collect your hamper."

He was both very gracious and proud.

"This is our lovely chapel, where we thank our Almighty God for all the wondrous gifts he bestows upon us."

"It's quite beautiful. Thank you for showing me a lovely sanctuary in which to collect one's thoughts."

"Exactly. It is where we find peace and a connection with our maker. Have you taken the Lord Jesus into your own heart Alkina?"

My response surprised me; Nan and her mother would have been impressed.

"Yes Father, I have."

Suddenly I had to leave.

"Thank you so much. It's a long drive and I should be starting back."

"Of course; we shall go via the kitchen."

I stowed the hamper in the back. Simon had been overgenerous.

"May God go with you! Now be of good cheer; your brother is in good hands."

I held my breath for the hug.

"Thank you Father David. I shall enjoy the hamper."

The balmy air in the valley hummed with insects and a soft breeze gently rocked the trees. I waved as I drove through the gate.

A Snifter with Vladimir

Politics ran in our family; at least my parents talked about it a lot, as did my wife and I, and for a short time, I dreamed of becoming a politician. This would have been for a variety of reasons. There was once a well-known political figure who lived in our street; so that may have had something to do with it, a nice chap, who, after a few ups and downs in life, did very well.

Then again, you know how it is with school children, and through them, I became friendly with another father in the neighborhood, who, at the time, was having a huge political career and went on to eventually become the Prime Minister. With friends like that, I had the right background, or we should more correctly say, I thought I had. The mistake I made was not to set my sights on it early in my life; and when I did, not to take it seriously enough. The trick is you have to live and breathe "the party", which I would agree can be a difficult thing to do.

I suppose that, like most candidates, I had attended my fair share of party meetings, which can be guaranteed to deaden the thinking processes of even the keenest stalwart. But, it is no good rushing in and saying to the party members, "Here I am, God's gift to the party, and the electorate; now you must all rally around and choose me to run."

Not at all; it does not work like that; I think it is a bit like nurturing a child. You have to bring them along and slowly, and rally them behind you. You know, you have to muck in for the long haul, do the menial tasks, and kiss all the dear old ladies, whom I belatedly discovered were the real power that drove the party. That is a little unfair; they didn't actually drive it anywhere; they nagged and prodded it in the general direction they wanted it to go.

I harbor the thought that perhaps having driven their husbands to scale the dizzy heights, they now needed other things to do. I am sure you understand, and I hypothesize that with enough dear old ladies behind you, a candidate would have a good chance of an illustrious career and might even go on to become the Prime Minister.

So the very next time you see our PM grandstanding over something grave and very macho, say an issue like the ordering of new fighters for the Air Force or battleships for the Navy, just remember that it is being done because a sufficient number of dear old ladies said that it should be. And why not? At least they take an interest. My complaint is that nobody ever mentioned them to me, so my chances of becoming the party's candidate were doomed from the start.

"Oh, he is so nice," they said of one of the other candidates, "just lovely; always offers the cakes and sandwiches around; so polite; and he comes in early and does the heavy lifting. It is a great help, you know, what with having to rearrange the tables and chairs. I honestly don't know what we would have done without him."

With that kind of personal following to challenge, only the insane would have kept going. I admit that I enjoyed the experience; but believe me, had I known then what I do now, I would not have stuck my toe in the water in the first place.

The thing is, there are those moments when you actually fantasize about winning, and jetting off to international conferences, and sharing the odd convivial sherry or two with Baroness Thatcher. It is heady stuff, and maybe sharing a few decent malts with Tony or George W, or a couple of snifters of really good Russian vodka with Vladimir. Thoughts like that can be a real come on to a susceptible personality like me.

Now, what you have to realize is that those world leaders have all been through the routine, which is how they became past masters at handling world affairs in the first place. They know perfectly well that if they can handle a bunch of old ladies who run a branch of their party, then handling the odd recalcitrant national leader is just a breeze.

Of course, being in the race to be chosen as the party's candidate to run in a particular seat at the next election puts an enormous strain on relationships. You have to drag your wife or partner around to function after function, and encourage them to laugh hilariously at even remotely amusing things uttered by perfect strangers, and anyone else whom you believe could be even of the slightest importance.

This is all about "getting the numbers", and before you know, you have been caught up in an endless round of meetings called for the benefit of the party faithful. These give them the opportunity to look you over as you pretend being a politician. Mind you, it gathers its own momentum, because they think the whole thing is a huge lark.

They propel you on with much backslapping and encouragement, as if they just might come good with a vote for you. They do this, while knowing all the while which of the candidates has already been given the nod, and has had all the votes tied up for months. So you make pretty speeches about how you see things, before you take questions from the floor. Foolishly, I thought I handled that part of it well, as, being a real estate auctioneer, I rather fancied myself in front of a crowd.

Being chosen as the party's candidate would have been a really big deal, they would have a vast army behind them as they sallied forth to carry the seat and become part of the next government. If I remember rightly, each branch in the electorate had members on the selection panel, and in addition, there were a few heavyweights from the head office, who attended on the big day. Any candidate worth their salt would have found out who was likely to be on the selection panel, and have been courting and entertaining them for months, all of which makes good politics. It might be that a corporation or a group of influential citizens will swing behind a candidate and look after their funding and the promotional side of it.

However, some of us do need a little time; and all of a sudden, like someone who has just found religion, I realized the awesome voting power of all those dear little old ladies I had been so foolishly ignoring. All those owners of purple—or was it blue—hair and those carefully crafted permanent waves, who stood in the background and sipped on cups of tea and chatted nicely to one another. A little late, you might say, but I was like a gold prospector who had just discovered a lode.

I came on like an avaricious salesman selling complete packages for a slick money-making scheme. I courted them on the way to and from the meetings, or any time I got the opportunity. I am embarrassed to recall, that like a chameleon, I had changed my colors, and my attitude, in an even bigger way. So much so, that I often found myself making two trips to collect a car load of those dear elderly ladies to drive them to and from a meeting.

Those in the know would have been quietly amused by all this carry-on, and very satisfied that they were witnessing all the intrigue and drama of democracy being played out before them. It was a bit like being an undercover agent, as during the campaign, no candidate told the others what they were doing. Indeed, they pretended they never had a chance, and they were not doing any behind-the-scenes campaigning at all.

But all the time, they had teams of supporters working the phones and sending out a continuous barrage of direct mail. Frantic, and as the day of reckoning drew closer, things began to heat up as I fielded last-minute phone calls to find out what I felt about this or that issue. It was nice that in a friendly fashion, many on the selection panel called to wish me well.

My wife had kept an inscrutable demeanor during the campaign, and when the day arrived, having put up with me strutting around the house for weeks, spouting the most inane political clichés, she and the children wished me good luck. Only official observers and those on the selection panel were allowed into the venue. It was going to be a long day, and in a last desperate flurry, or so it seems now, I collected a last car full of... I am sure you know who, and away we went.

You could say I was dripping charm, and a few miles away from the venue, somehow the conversation had strayed from myself, as the potential, overwhelmingly successful candidate, and unfortunately switched to discussing the much-rumored favorite candidate.

"Goodness me, they hosted a beautiful dinner," said one old dear. "So generous, and my flowers were simply gorgeous. I also received a very nice card to thank me for attending," she explained breathlessly.

"Ladies, I intend to fight for increased pensions when I get in," I parried, "and I am going to work like hell to get an increase in the allowable income before the pension is effected," I canvassed with some vigor.

There was absolutely no response from any of my passengers.

"Did I tell you I have an invitation to join the new member for lunch in Parliament House?" said the passenger beside me.

"Yes, wasn't that nice? So did we," said the back seat, in an angelic, yet final, morale-sapping chorus.

Part IV -
Saying Goodbyes

A Very Fine Man

When I was a suburban real estate agent, I once attended a funeral, as a favor to a friend, as a sort of guest mourner. I have always thought it a very strange happening, so let me explain the circumstances. The way it unfolded was unintentional, particularly as I had never met the deceased, who, incidentally, was lying in final repose in a mahogany casket in the living room.

One of the things that I discovered when I arrived in Sydney was that young men who came from the country, as I had, often gravitated to selling real estate out in the suburbs. Perhaps it was because they were used to working relatively unsupervised, and welcomed the space and freedom of being outdoors. I think that once they got over their initial shyness, their hard work and straightforward manner worked very much in their favor. The best salesman I ever worked with was a former pig farmer whose modus operandi was very simple, for he just opened the commercial telephone book under 'Boarding Houses' and sallied forth to meet the owners.

Another was a very intelligent and industrious young man who had left home after one of those growing up rifts with his farmer father. This chap arrived in a huff, and then commenced to string together some of the biggest and smartest commercial deals ever seen in the city. But for myself, after a period of diving in and out of suburban houses, I found a lucrative niche selling factories, large building sites, office buildings, shops, and so on. Perhaps one of the main reasons I went down that path may have been the strong competition from one of the other salesmen. He was also from the country and had the uncanny ability to produce a second cousin, or a distant aunt, in the most sought-after street of the best suburb. It happened time and again, and having got a roll on with one sale, the surrounding vendors naturally asked for him.

Yet, sometimes success just arrives when you least expect it, as it did on this particular day when a shabbily-dressed man arrived on our doorstep to inspect some property. Having worked as a pick-and-shovel man myself, I could see he had come straight from a construction site. Meanwhile my more genteel city brethren had taken a quick look and disappeared out the back of the shop.

Off we went, and after the usual getting-to-know-you chatter and driving about, we hit upon a row of rundown shops in a nearby suburb, and in a young salesman's enthusiasm, I said, "Why not take one of these, do it up, and then we can sell it again?"

"Not a bad idea," he said, as we wandered in and out of the deserted shops.

"Which one would you like?"

"I'll make an offer for the lot," he replied, and suddenly I had stumbled upon a wonderful client with whom I did business over the years.

The industry was a lot more relaxed than it is today. There was none of this glassy-eyed singing the corporate song at high-powered breakfast meetings, or wearing the regulation company tie and blazer. The house listing sheet might say, "Mrs. Brown has cards on Thursday afternoons, and does not mind inspections. Bozo likes to be scratched behind the ears and can stay inside; the wardrobe in the second bedroom is included. The front door key is under the small cacti pot on the front porch." Perhaps everyone had more spare time to relax.

There was the occasion when I was asked to put a price on a home down in General Monash Street, number fifty-two or, as the girl had written down, "The one with the two white chimneys and the green front fence." When I arrived, the front door was wide open, and after knocking politely, I went in. Out in the pleasant living room overlooking the rear garden, a ladies' luncheon was in full swing. I was very cordially greeted; was seated, and found myself hoeing into a delicious chicken casserole and having an amicable chat with some very nice ladies, one of whom was the hostess. Somewhere in the conversation, it became clear that I was in the wrong house, which produced much merriment and the fulsome invitation to stay for wine trifle and coffee.

I once worked under a very pleasant manager, who liked to hold his sales meetings in the refreshing atmosphere of the local sailing club, where on Monday mornings, we would gather unobtrusively around a table in a corner of the dining room, where, undisturbed by phones and the usual disruptions of a busy real estate office, we could bring ourselves up to date with where we were with our vendors and their properties. This was done by thumbing through the listings, which comprised a page of detail in a loose-leafed book. One day, I was having a convivial drink at the same club, when the bar steward happened to ask me if I was one of the meter readers who met there on Monday mornings. When I told my boss, he was very tickled, and from then on, we dubbed ourselves the Meter Readers' Club.

I was never sure whether I was just lucky, or if the people I dealt with were more friendly and tolerant than people are today. I fancy they were. Certainly the talk in the office was warm toward and protective of our owners, and I do not remember law suits or complaints to the Real Estate Institute. But times change, and nor do I remember ever reading gossipy items in the paper about who bought a particular home and what they paid for it. We regarded that information as confidential. But like everyone else, we did make our mistakes. There was the time when I had a hand as a salesman in a very successful auction of a magnificent waterfront home, and to this day, the buyer and I remain friends.

That happened at a time when solicitors were perhaps put on too high a pedestal, and I knew she had employed the best, certainly one of the more expensive in Sydney. It was their job to vet the purchaser's contract on her behalf. I can still picture her at the auction, giving her lawyer a sharp prod with her umbrella when she thought he was not bidding vigorously enough. But in the end, the house was knocked down to her, and she was as pleased as you like; and it was months later that we met in the street.

"Oh", she said, "my dear Mr. Gibson, although I love our new home, I have to say you never told me it was not connected to the sewage system."

"Isn't it Mrs. Hanwood?" I was genuinely astonished, recalling that obviously, for very good reason, my salesman's copy of the owner's contract had never included a water and drainage plan. Still doubting, we went to her home to check it out; and of course it was not; but that was as far as it ever went?

It helped to always be forthright. There was once a bitter marital split and as far as an agent or a buyer was concerned, the property boundaries were clearly marked by the existing fencing. However, that was not the case, as there was a right of way in favor of a neighbor that had not been disclosed to me, and which ran straight across the front lawn. However, in one of life's great ironies, the buyer just happened to be a prominent legal expert in the field, and of course quickly discovered the problem, much to my embarrassment. After my delivery of a huge bunch of flowers to him and his wife, my humble apologies and a difficult negotiation to unscramble the damage, the sale went through, and that was the end of the matter.

We enjoyed the camaraderie of our occupation, and because most of us did six days straight, we usually went out for lunch on Fridays. These lunches were something of an institution, during which there was a lot of catching up and a great deal of good humor.

But I was telling you of that funeral. One Thursday, a friend rang to say he doubted he would be able to make the lunch, and asked if I could come to the funeral of one of his former clients. It was to be held the next morning, after which we could endeavor to join the others for lunch. A short time after we arrived at the home, it became very clear that apart from the widow, we were the only mourners. Mrs. Shaunessey was Australian-Irish, a robust lady who came from the country somewhere out in the Central West, which was the connection with my friend. It is also fair to say she liked a tipple. The first thing I can recall is having a malt whisky put into my hand, one of many to come, while she talked in brave but grief-stricken terms of her late husband, as we stood around his, fortunately, closed casket, waiting for the funeral director to arrive.

After the service and internment, we were joined by the priest, a pleasant and well meaning man, who, by his prominently-veined nose, I suspected might also enjoy a tipple. However, as the morning progressed, our usual Friday lunch was clearly out of contention. There was no way we could desert the widow, who had insisted we return to her home for a wake, one of the few I have ever attended.

Thus, I found myself in animated conversation with the priest, while eating dainty sandwiches and drinking malt whiskey, and doing my best to avoid any mention of the dear departed, about whom I knew absolutely nothing. Malt whiskey, I believe, has a tendency to make one drop one's guard, as I think happened to me, because no matter how hard I tried, I could not avoid the subject when it came up.

"Michael Shaunessey was a devoted husband and father," said the priest, "and you were a close friend I believe?"

"He was a very fine man, Father," I said reverently.

"That he was," said the widow, who had joined us. "Let us drink a toast to Michael Shaunessey, a loving husband, a wonderful friend, and a very fine man," she added, which of course we did, as well as another and another, until in, what seemed like no time at all, it was dark.

Many months later, I was in my office when a plump man with an Irishman's face came in and introduced himself as Terrence Shaunessey, and I am afraid to say I did not immediately make the connection, or not as quickly as I should have.

"I was very distressed," he explained, "that I could not get across for my father's funeral. However, as soon as I heard the news, I had chest pains and was advised not to attempt the long flight from Canada. I just wanted to say thank you for looking after my mother, and to meet and shake the hand of a friend of my father."

Over a cup of tea and my great trepidation, he produced a framed photo of a man I had never met before in my life. "I would like you to accept this as a memento of my father," he said.

"Thank you very much Mr. Shaunessey," I said as convincingly as I could. "He was a very fine man."

Goodbye Elsie Pascoe

The passing of Elsie Pascoe was just one of those occurrences that happen on the very fringes of one's life. I had never met her, although I was the chief and only mourner at her funeral service. I would think "attendee" would better describe my being there at all. This may sound callous and disrespectful, so let me explain how this charade had come about.

I imagine you will have heard that over-told, and, in my view, juvenile and demeaning story of the Pommy jackeroo, who arrives on a huge, Australian, outback cattle station where he is given a horse to ride which no one, not even the crack stockmen, has been able to stay on. Of course, he not only stays on but demonstrates complete mastery over the horse, as if doing so was nothing out of the ordinary. This type of story may go somewhere to explain what is, in my view, the stupid Australian practice of giving "a lesson in life" to young people who are just starting out in their new careers.

This helps to explain what happened to me when I became the newest recruit to join a much-venerated old firm of trustees and executors, who shall remain nameless. This career move delighted my mother, who, with considerable entrepreneurial flair, ran a suburban corner-shop grocery business, and used to proudly tell her friends and customers, that her youngest son had recently joined a highly respected company in the city. Indeed I had, and the old firm is still located precisely where it was when I left it many years ago, that is in the business heart of the city. However, in hindsight, it seems to me that they had a tradition of 'blooding', for want of a better word, their new recruits; and, in doing so, displayed that same perverse style of Australian humor.

Not long after I joined, I was formally summoned to see my immediate superior, a Mr. Allworthy, a man who was steeped in the traditions of the old firm. This meeting had a serious tenor to it, because, as the executors and trustees of her estate, I was instructed to represent the company at the late Elsie Pascoe's funeral service. With that, I was given a large brown envelope containing what I found to be a very shabby, black, mourning tie, which not only looked disgusting, but was very out-of-fashion. I could barely believe that, as a young man on the way up, I could be expected to wear such an awful tie to her funeral, which was to be held the following morning. I was further instructed that a chauffeur-driven car from the funeral director would call at the office to fetch me.

Upon further inspection at home, I found the tie was covered with mildew stains. That night, I did my best to sponge it clean, but dreaded wearing it as I thought it looked ridiculous. The next morning, I delayed putting it on until just before the funeral director's car was due.

At this time, the older members of staff, and anyone else who knew what was about to happen, had gathered to watch me leave wearing what I took to be the "official company mourning tie." The limousine driver was a friendly sort of fellow, and we chatted as we drove through the suburbs, and before long, I found myself seated toward the back of the spooky chapel of a desolate-looking funeral home. Across the front, and in large copperplate signage, a sign announced that I was attending the "Purcell Bros, Funeral Parlor."

Yet, there was something vaguely familiar about that name. The atmosphere in the chapel was somber, and obviously meant to convey to the most light-hearted visitor that the end was nigh. There were the expected church pews, much dark wood, white lace, and polished brass. I had two thoughts—how to get out of there, and to take off that disgusting tie.

Out in the front, Elsie Pascoe rested in her casket between two enormous, highly-polished brass urns, filled with a bunch of white lilies. While I contemplated the loneliness of her unmourned passing, her funeral service got underway when the piped music began. As I recall, it was a flat, tuneless dirge, which was bound to hasten any wavering soul toward their final destination.

Then a young man in clerical collar and surplice appeared and made the sign of the cross over the casket, and, in a low voice, intoned something incomprehensible to me before he disappeared to one side. Then there appeared a pale-faced young man, dressed in long grey tails and morning trousers, who could have been a character straight out of a Victorian melodrama. This figure was scurrying down the aisle in my direction, and as he drew nearer, his face seemed familiar.

"Sir, we are most deeply sorry at your sad loss," he said, most solicitously, while bending down to my ear, "and would, sir, care to say a final farewell to the dear departed before we seal the casket?"

"No thank you," I replied, thinking it was a bit too late for Elsie and me to strike up an acquaintance. But during this exchange, there had been the mutual recognition that we knew each other from our school days of only a few years before, and that we were surprised at this unlikely meeting. He was none other than Arnold Purcell, who had been a pretty good middle-distance runner, and had been in the same year.

"Geoffrey, old mate, you are representing the executors?"

"Yes, I only joined them a few weeks ago."

"So you are not mourning the deceased?"

"No, I did not know her."

"Good. We can get together for lunch after the formalities."

Thus resumed an old school friendship, which would have been helped along by my being seen as a potential source of business for the Purcell Brothers' funeral parlor. By the time the hearse had left for the internment, Arnold had changed into street clothes and the first thing he said was "where in the hell did you get that crappy tie?" And I became aware that I had been well and truly inducted into the firm

I never told anyone in our office that I had been whisked away to a very swish restaurant. There, Arnold insisted it would buck up our spirits if we each had a dozen fresh Sydney rock oysters for starters, washed down by one or two cold beers. Or how that was followed by a very tender filet mignon served with one of the most luscious red wines I had ever tasted.

Arnold was great company, and we caught up with what we had done since leaving school, and I thought it was a terrific lunch. But I was unused to such high living, and I offered to share the cost. "Don't even think about it," he said, "I have strict instructions from my dad that this is a very fitting way for us to farewell Elsie Pascoe."

Farewell, Dear Sister!

Time heals, and I am prompted to write this after watching some interesting television journalism on the shocking toll of breast cancer.

On the day of our sister's funeral, my brother and I met at the airport, did our ticketing, and boarded our flight. Our chatter had a false bravado about it, as we tried to shake off the sadness of that day and lift each other's spirits. Perhaps, for the uninitiated, I should reflect that there is a period in a person's life in which far too often you have to pause to mark the passing of those you love, a ritual which is as necessary and as sure, as the setting of the sun at the end of a day. We shared a drink with another passenger, a friendly and entertaining barrister my brother knew, also on his way to Melbourne, and during the conversation, my brother and I discovered that we had been charged a lot more for our tickets than he had. This led to a lively and amusing debate about the bastardry and trickiness of airline ticketing, and to us seeking and getting a refund upon reaching our destination, all of which would have been a light-hearted and welcome diversion before the funeral.

As all this happened long ago, it is now quite comfortable for me to write about it. May I continue by saying that I have always thought of my elder sister as being angelic, for she was one of those people who regard their time here on earth as an opportunity to serve others? She had four children of her own, and adopted her last two, which I think sums her up better than anything I can write. Suffice to say she was greatly loved by a great many people, some of whom were to later demonstrate their regard for her in their own inimitable way, as you will shortly see.

Let me turn the clock back to when she was a girl in her early teens and attended an exclusive girls' school, and came back from a school camp in emotional turmoil. Her camp had been run by a missionary-style evangelical group, and under them, she had undergone a profound religious conversion. I might mention that my brother and I went through the same experience, although the effect on us was short-lived. I only write of it as background, as this is not the moment to enter into a discussion as to the right or wrong of this type of brainwashing, or of foisting the guilt of sin upon my innocent and unsuspecting sister. However, she married a Church of England curate, and in a practical way, went on to live her religious convictions to the end of her all too short life.

But to return to that day, my brother had first to attend to some business in the heart of Melbourne, and in an act of practical friendship, his associates took us out for a very nice lunch before the service. The only mitigating thing that I can say about a death from cancer is that the family and loved ones they leave behind usually have time to prepare for it. Her husband and children appeared to be coping well. How much of this was bravura, I could not say, but I do remember feeling that my tears were letting the side down, and my brother later mentioned that he had felt the same way.

I cannot remember the precise details of that day, or of her service, or what I might have said, especially to her children. There were many parishioners among the mourners, many of whom came up to my brother and I to express their sorrow, and I can recall someone telling me the funeral director had very kindly donated his services. There were masses of flowers, and it was abundantly clear she had been held in high esteem by her community, and was going to be missed.

Just before the cortège left for the internment, the latter part of the service was held in the grounds of the chapel, and it involved a most impressive new forest green hearse, which bore her flower draped coffin. This impressive machine stood in a pride of place just outside the chapel. Paraded on either side was an honor guard of the funeral director's staff, who were dressed in matching forest-green jackets. A very nice tribute, I thought, when, to my shock, there was the sound of hydraulics, and the side of the hearse opened, and our dear sister's coffin was lifted outwards and upwards until it was suspended high in the air. Then, in a display of mechanical dexterity, and the latest in funeral director's equipment, it was swiveled around three hundred and sixty degrees in a kind of farewell salute to her family, friends, and to the world, before returning to its original position, and her cortège slowly moved off.

The Gift

When Mrs. Thelma Cotter Chaseling took that final step and entered the great beyond, and became the Estate of the late Thelma Cotter Chaseling, she had no idea of the chain of events she was setting in motion. Unwittingly, of course, as we never knew each other; nonetheless, she wove herself into my life. She is still there today, in distant memory. I mean no disrespect for her or her descendants, who would be as unaware and as innocent as I was; but nonetheless, whether we like it or not, we share that link.

Thelma left behind a new set of lawn bowls, a reasonable set of golf clubs, rooms full of bric-a-brac, some cash at the bank and a well-performing portfolio of shares in listed companies. There was also a four-door Ford sedan with only about forty thousand on the clock, and a substantial home, and I have to say without getting carried away that her home was in one of the nicer suburbs of Sydney. All in all, I imagined her as being a nice lady, and I think we would have got on, although, as this is many years on, I must say I don't care for lawn bowls at all.

Years ago, I had a respectable position in the city, with a solid and most reputable firm of Trustees and Executors. My mother's influence, no doubt, as her father had been a proud member of the Metropolitan Water Sewerage and Drainage Board, and she was very keen on me working in a similar, "reputable organization". My grandmother had a blown-up portrait of my grandfather wearing a well-cut suit, with gold chain across his waistcoat. He had a large, bushy, carefully-shaped waxed moustache, which stretched to a point far out and on either side of his mouth. My grandfather also wore a most dignified, if posed, expression, all set off by a tie, a tie pin, and a stiff white butterfly-winged collar.

But to return to my position in the trust company, presumably to this day, locked away in a dingy vault somewhere there is a thick leather-bound book of very high quality lined pages, which in my day was known as *The Trust Book*. My hope is that it will remain locked away and never be looked at again. Because "written in pen-and-ink", is not quite correct, more accurate to say "scrawled and blotched in my illegible hand", is the record of my administration of Thelma's estate. This may just as well have been recorded in an obscure Swahili dialect, as no one could read it then, and I am absolutely sure no one would be able to read it now.

My handwriting was, and still is, so illegible that I once wrote a letter to some dear friends of mine, whom I promptly avoided; being miffed, they did not have the courtesy to reply. However, all was put right when we next met at a mutual friend's function, and the husband sheepishly replied they had not been able to read it; so you see.

It was, and still is, so bad that I should have been a doctor. What I discovered, and I am sure you will have noticed, is that when you go to the pharmacist with your prescription, the dispenser always asks, "And what seems to be the matter with you?" The answer, of course, gives them that vital clue as to what your script should say, even if it doesn't. So what is on my mind is the knowledge that there are pages and pages of my handwriting locked away, which deal with Thelma's affairs, about which no one has ever been able to read.

Nonetheless, I did well at the trust company and was promoted as a sort of 'outside man' to the extent that if there were no mourners for the deceased, that task would fall upon me. Wearing a somber tie, and having been collected in a chauffeured limousine, I would attend the service and ensure everything was as it should have been. And one day, I was sitting at my desk, adding up long columns of figures, when I received a phone call. It was the man from the cremation company, wanting to know if I wanted Thelma's ashes, "scattered to the four winds of heaven". But when I discovered the exorbitant cost of simply going outside, and standing on the windward side of a garden bed during a stiff north easterly, which blows in Sydney most of the time anyway, and letting them go, I declined.

A month later, I received a rather terse letter from the same gentleman, to the effect that as no member of the family had collected Thelma's ashes, "would our company, as the executor of her estate, kindly arrange for someone to do so?" Which is how I came to be travelling with a large square box, with two layers of brown paper wrapped around it, on the "all stops, two fifteen", coming from the north shore, and pulling into Wynyard Station in the heart of the city.

In her then state, I would say Thelma was about twelve inches square and weighed around two kilograms. I quite enjoyed my job, and the truth was I liked getting out of the office, and on the way back, with her ashes under one arm, I indulged in a little window shopping.

I should pause to explain that for many years, I was embarrassed by the memory of my conduct with members of the opposite sex, in those wayward years prior to marriage. It is only now with daughters of my own that I have discovered that perhaps those feelings may have been overdone. My then girlfriend was a very nice young lady named Jennifer Guilthorpe, of whom I was very fond, as I recall, as she was of me. She and I always held hands everywhere we went, and her mother made us delicious sandwiches filled with chicken breast or choice red salmon with lettuce and mayonnaise, all nicely wrapped in foil.

Jennifer and I could spend the whole weekend holding hands and finding places where we could, I hesitate to say, *snog*; but they do it everywhere today without a care in the world. It would have been outside a well-known gentleman's outfitter, known as "Hunts", where, with Thelma firmly under my arm, I was gazing with some interest and fantasizing about what I would buy, if I could afford to, when a familiar hand slid into mine, and my love had unexpectedly joined me. Naturally, we went to a coffee shop and sat at a table as far away from the street as we could find, and with Thelma safely on the floor, we drank coffee and held hands.

As it was to be Jennifer's birthday in a few days, the contents of my square parcel raised her expectations. There was also the problem that I had never exactly told her what I did; indeed, rather foolishly, I made out that I was more important than I was, and there was absolutely no way I was going to tell her where I had been or what was in the box. Of course, I kidded her; and the more I did, the more her curiosity rose, and the more she squeezed my hand, as we gazed adoringly at each other.

Knowing I was getting in over my head, I looked at my watch, as if I had to be somewhere in hurry. But before we got up, she said, "Truly Geoffrey dear, I really won't mind, you can tell me, but I am almost sure it is a portable radio." In a moment, we were out in the street, and about to go in opposite directions. Then she looked up with the fondest expression and said, "It is only so nobody else buys me one as well."

At last, completely cornered, I gave her a farewell peck and whispered, "It contains a client's ashes."

"Oh, you are hysterical!" she said, literally collapsing on the footpath. "I can't wait to tell my mum."

About the Author.

If you will step inside my mind briefly, I will try to explain my world for you. I am once again a boy again in the years of the Second World War and living with my mother and an older brother and sister. We live in a flat on the shore of Sydney Harbor in Double Bay, where my mother successfully runs a suburban grocery shop while my father is overseas fighting Hitler and someone called the "Nips". What concerns me is that my friend Dicky is a much better swimmer than I am, and that I love a little girl named Carroll in my class. The only time I wear shoes is when I go to school.

An anti-submarine boom is stretched across the harbor, and when a Japanese sub randomly lobs shells at Sydney, we shelter under the kitchen table. Large British and American warships glide in and out, and for the first time I taste tomato soup onboard a huge British battleship. Our introductions to Coca Cola and sticks of gum comes later. With apologies, "the Yanks", and we never call them anything else, maroon their little timber motorboats they hire to take their girls out for a day on the harbor, on the mud bank in front of our place. Then they tip us with Coke and sticks of gum when we wade out and push them off. The Yanks, their Coke, sticks of gum and Hopalong Cassidy are our heroes.

Those years are not so long ago in my mind. There were no supermarkets or television, and our King and Queen lived far away in London, and in our hour of peril, for the first time since settlement we loosened the apron strings. It is high time we untied them completely.

So what have we lost?

I think we have lost a lot more than we realize, certainly the ability to converse with each other and to amuse ourselves. For me, apart from sport and the news, most of what passes for television is bilge. Is it too unkind to say we are losing our sense of humor? If we are, I blame it on TV prompts like canned laughter, you have seen and heard them yourself, hysterical laughter blaring from the set, over a dialogue that is not even remotely funny. For I remember the cut and thrust of lively and amusing dinner time conversation. Even more Orwellian, I feel we are in danger of having what we see and hear slanted and controlled by an unseen, unelected and uncontrollable power.

What have we gained?

The greatest gift of all, a close friend. I refer of course to our genuine and enduring affection for America.

I feel it is a great privilege to still be hale and healthy, and I have written these stories, particularly "The Taciturn Man", as a tribute to the father I barely knew when I was a boy. The rest of this collection are reminiscences, and have been written to entertain the reader. I hope they do.

The World Voices Series

This series highlights the best English-language autobiography, fiction, and poetry of diverse voices from Africa, Asia, the Caribbean, and South America.

Because All Is Not Lost: Verse on Grief
By Sweta Srivastava Vikram

Kaleidoscope: An Asian Journey with Colors.
By Sweta Srivastava Vikram

The Blue Fairy and other tales of transcendence
By Ernest Dempsey

Iraq Through a Bullet Hole: A Civilian Wikileaks
by Issam Jameel

The Road-Shaped Heart
by Nick Purdon

Beyond the Scent of Sorrow
By Sweta Srivastava Vikram

The Taciturn Man and other tales of Australia
by Geoffrey Gibson

MODERN
HISTORY
PRESS

from Modern History Press
http://www.modernhistorypress.com/world-voices/